W9-CFV-090

JAN 3 0 2015

OPPOSING VIEWPOINTS® SERIES

The Republican Party

Other Books of Related Interest:

Opposing Viewpoints Series

The Democratic Party

Government Gridlock

US Foreign Policy

Voting Rights

At Issue Series

The Affordable Care Act

Negative Campaigning

Current Controversies Series

Immigration

Politics and Religion

"Congress shall make no law . . . abridging the freedom of speech, or of the press."

First Amendment to the US Constitution

The basic foundation of our democracy is the First Amendment guarantee of freedom of expression. The Opposing Viewpoints series is dedicated to the concept of this basic freedom and the idea that it is more important to practice it than to enshrine it.

The Republican Party

Noah Berlatsky, Book Editor

GREENHAVEN PRESS

A part of Gale, Cengage Learning

Farmington Hills, Mich • San Francisco • New York • Waterville, Maine
Meriden, Conn • Mason, Ohio • Chicago

Patricia Coryell, *Vice President & Publisher, New Products & GVRL*
Douglas Dentino, *Manager, New Products*
Judy Galens, *Acquisitions Editor*

For more information, contact:
Greenhaven Press
27500 Drake Rd.
Farmington Hills, MI 48331-3535
Or you can visit our Internet site at gale.cengage.com

Articles in Greenhaven Press anthologies are often edited for length to meet page requirements. In addition, original titles of these works are changed to clearly present the main thesis and to explicitly indicate the author's opinion. Every effort is made to ensure that Greenhaven Press accurately reflects the original intent of the authors. Every effort has been made to trace the owners of copyrighted material.

Cover Image copyright © Jacob Hamblin/Shutterstock.com.

LIBRARY OF CONGRESS CATALOGING-IN-PUBLICATION DATA

The Republican Party / Noah Berlatsky, book editor.
    pages cm. -- -- (Opposing viewpoints) Summary: "Opposing Viewpoints: The Republican Party: Opposing Viewpoints is the leading source for libraries and classrooms in need of current-issue materials. The viewpoints are selected from a wide range of highly respected sources and publications"-- Provided by publisher.
    Includes bibliographical references and index.
    ISBN 978-0-7377-7284-5 (hardback) -- ISBN 978-0-7377-7285-2 (paperback)
    1. Republican Party (U.S. : 1854-) 2. United States--Politics and government--Juvenile literature. I. Berlatsky, Noah.
    JK2356.R32 2015
    324.2734--dc23

                                                    2014030237

Contents

Chapter 3: What Issues Divide Republicans?

Chapter 4: What Issues Surround the Tea Party?

Why Consider Opposing Viewpoints?

> *"The only way in which a human being can make some approach to knowing the whole of a subject is by hearing what can be said about it by persons of every variety of opinion and studying all modes in which it can be looked at by every character of mind. No wise man ever acquired his wisdom in any mode but this."*
>
> John Stuart Mill

In our media-intensive culture it is not difficult to find differing opinions. Thousands of newspapers and magazines and dozens of radio and television talk shows resound with differing points of view. The difficulty lies in deciding which opinion to agree with and which "experts" seem the most credible. The more inundated we become with differing opinions and claims, the more essential it is to hone critical reading and thinking skills to evaluate these ideas. Opposing Viewpoints books address this problem directly by presenting stimulating debates that can be used to enhance and teach these skills. The varied opinions contained in each book examine many different aspects of a single issue. While examining these conveniently edited opposing views, readers can develop critical thinking skills such as the ability to compare and contrast authors' credibility, facts, argumentation styles, use of persuasive techniques, and other stylistic tools. In short, the Opposing Viewpoints Series is an ideal way to attain the higher-level thinking and reading skills so essential in a culture of diverse and contradictory opinions.

In addition to providing a tool for critical thinking, Opposing Viewpoints books challenge readers to question their own strongly held opinions and assumptions. Most people form their opinions on the basis of upbringing, peer pressure, and personal, cultural, or professional bias. By reading carefully balanced opposing views, readers must directly confront new ideas as well as the opinions of those with whom they disagree. This is not to argue simplistically that everyone who reads opposing views will—or should—change his or her opinion. Instead, the series enhances readers' understanding of their own views by encouraging confrontation with opposing ideas. Careful examination of others' views can lead to the readers' understanding of the logical inconsistencies in their own opinions, perspective on why they hold an opinion, and the consideration of the possibility that their opinion requires further evaluation.

Evaluating Other Opinions

To ensure that this type of examination occurs, Opposing Viewpoints books present all types of opinions. Prominent spokespeople on different sides of each issue as well as well-known professionals from many disciplines challenge the reader. An additional goal of the series is to provide a forum for other, less known, or even unpopular viewpoints. The opinion of an ordinary person who has had to make the decision to cut off life support from a terminally ill relative, for example, may be just as valuable and provide just as much insight as a medical ethicist's professional opinion. The editors have two additional purposes in including these less known views. One, the editors encourage readers to respect others' opinions—even when not enhanced by professional credibility. It is only by reading or listening to and objectively evaluating others' ideas that one can determine whether they are worthy of consideration. Two, the inclusion of such viewpoints encourages the important critical thinking skill of objectively evaluating an author's credentials and bias. This evaluation will illuminate an author's reasons for taking a particular stance on an issue and will aid in readers' evaluation of the author's ideas.

It is our hope that these books will give readers a deeper understanding of the issues debated and an appreciation of the complexity of even seemingly simple issues when good and honest people disagree. This awareness is particularly important in a democratic society such as ours in which people enter into public debate to determine the common good. Those with whom one disagrees should not be regarded as enemies but rather as people whose views deserve careful examination and may shed light on one's own.

Thomas Jefferson once said that "difference of opinion leads to inquiry, and inquiry to truth." Jefferson, a broadly educated man, argued that "if a nation expects to be ignorant and free . . . it expects what never was and never will be." As individuals and as a nation, it is imperative that we consider the opinions of others and examine them with skill and discernment. The Opposing Viewpoints series is intended to help readers achieve this goal.

David L. Bender and Bruno Leone,
Founders

Introduction

> "Dwight Eisenhower reduced national defense outlays by 28 percent from their 1953 Korean War peak. Presidents Richard Nixon and Gerald Ford went even further, cutting 37 percent from the defense budget after the Vietnam-era high in 1968. And President George H.W. Bush had cut 14 percent compared with the 1989 Cold War budget by the time he left office.

> "All these presidents were Republicans. Meanwhile, after adjusting for inflation, the most expensive defense budget in more than 60 years belongs to President Obama, a Democrat."
>
> *—Gordon Adams and*
> *Matthew Leatherman,*
> *"Five Myths About Defense Spending,"*
> Washington Post, *January 14, 2011*

Republicans have long been associated with enthusiastic support for military spending. Ronald Reagan, in particular, often seen as the guiding light of the current Republican Party, was known for his military buildup. Over his term from 1980 to 1988, "he had expanded the U.S. military budget to a staggering 43% increase over the total expenditure during the height of the Vietnam war," according to the article "Ronald Reagan's Military Buildup" at the United States History website. Defense spending reached a height of $456.5 billion in 1987 (in 2005 dollars) according to a June 9, 2004, article by Greg Schneider and Renae Merle in the *Washington Post*. Republican president George W. Bush followed in this tradition—as did Democratic president Barack Obama. By 2011, according to a July 6, 2011, article at the Center for American Progress website, "Total U.S. defense spending (in inflation-adjusted dollars) has increased so much over the past decade that it has reached levels not seen since World War II, when the United States had 12 million people under arms and waged wars on three continents."

However, in recent years, Republicans have begun to be conflicted about support for large amounts of military spending. The Tea Party movement in 2010 focused intensely on balancing the budget and fiscal responsibility but was also strongly opposed to increased taxation. Republicans do not want to vote for more revenue and want to balance the budget; the only way to do this is to reduce spending, and that may have to include military spending. As a result, according to a March 13, 2013, article by David Francis at the Fiscal Times website, "the Pentagon is no longer a GOP [Grand Old Party] sacred cow." Francis goes further and argues that there is actually a long tradition in the Republican Party of putting balanced budgets ahead of defense spending. He quotes Gordon Adams, a professor at American University, who points out that most major defense drawdowns, such as the one following World War II or the one following the Cold War, were presided over by Republican presidents. "There is a history here of Republicans being more concerned with the fiscal than they are about defense," Adams says.

That history continues today. Rand Paul, a senator from Kentucky and much discussed as a possible contender for the 2016 Republican presidential nomination, has spoken out repeatedly in favor of defense spending cuts. In a July 23, 2012, article at *Slate*, for example, David Weigel quotes Paul as saying in regard to defense spending, "I'm of the belief that nothing around you will ever be efficient unless the top line number is lower ... and if you really believe in savings in the military budget . . . you'd be forced to find the savings." Paul also argues for auditing the Pentagon and suggests that the military will never start moving toward greater efficiency unless defense spending is reduced.

Paul's stance remains very controversial within the Republican Party, however. In the same article where he discusses Rand Paul, David Weigel also quotes other Republican senators, including Kelly Ayotte of New Hampshire and Lindsey Graham of South Carolina, speaking out against any defense cuts. David Lawder, in a March 27, 2014, article at Reuters, quotes Representative Steve King of Iowa, a leading Tea Party Republican, advocating for *more* defense spending. "We need to send a message out of the White House and Congress that we're not going to be weak and keep cutting our military," King said. Lawder also notes that Russia's invasion of Ukraine in 2014 led many Republicans to renew calls for greater defense spending and resistance to defense cuts.

Matthew Cooper in a February 25, 2014, article for *Newsweek* suggests that "it's easy to picture a Republican primary in 2016 where the libertarian-minded Senator Rand Paul from Kentucky defends a smaller Army, while the likes of House member from Wisconsin Paul Ryan or former Florida governor Jeb Bush want a bigger force." However, not all commenters are convinced that the Republican Party is ready for a real debate on defense spending. Political scientist Jonathan Bernstein in a May 4, 2013, article at Salon.com argues that "there's just no way . . . that the people within the Republican Party who care about foreign policy and national security would easily accept Rand Paul." In Bernstein's view, Republican support for defense spending and intervention remains such that a candidate could not successfully run on a platform of reduced military action and cuts in defense.

Defense spending is just one topic of discussion among members of the Republican Party. *Opposing Viewpoints: The Republican Party* explores other important issues confronting the GOP in chapters titled "What Factors Affect Republican Electoral Chances?," "What Is the Relationship of Republicans to Important Voting Groups?," "What Issues Divide Republicans?," and "What Issues Surround the Tea Party?" Different authors offer varying viewpoints on the current status and future of the Republican Party.

OPPOSING
VIEWPOINTS®
SERIES

CHAPTER 1

What Factors Affect Republican Electoral Chances?

Chapter Preface

One important factor affecting a party's electoral chances is candidate quality. Recruiting qualified, popular candidates is essential to winning close elections. Over the last few election cycles, Republicans have lost a number of key congressional races when far right-wing, inexperienced candidates defeated more moderate, experienced candidates in Republican primaries and then went on to lose to Democrats in the general election. In 2010, for example, Sharron Angle defeated more moderate candidates in the Nevada Republican primary but then lost a close race to the very unpopular Senate majority leader Democrat Harry Reid. Similarly, in 2012 Todd Akin won the Republican Senate primary against several, more moderate candidates. During the campaign, however, Akin stirred controversy when he suggested that women who are raped rarely get pregnant as a result of the sexual assault. Even though he apologized for his remarks, his popularity plummeted. As a result, he was defeated by Democratic senator Claire McCaskill in the election.

Republicans seem poised to have similar problems in the future, according to a September 26, 2013, *National Journal* article by Alex Roarty. In Georgia, for example, Roarty predicted that Representative Paul Broun, who has called evolution a "lie from the pit of hell," had a serious chance of winning the Republican primary for a vacant Senate seat in 2014 but would have had difficulty in the general election against Democratic nominee Michelle Nunn, daughter of former senator Sam Nunn. (Broun lost in the 2014 Republican primary.) Republicans also faced potentially volatile primaries in Alaska, Iowa, Kentucky, and North Carolina. Democrats, on the other hand, were poised to have uneventful primaries and uncontroversial candidates in all of these states.

Republicans are trying to address these issues. A group called the Conservative Victory Project, associated with long-time Republican operative Karl Rove, intends to try to fund mainstream candidates and intervene in primaries against in-experienced or extreme candidates such as Angle and Akin. In a February 4, 2013, post at *Slate*, however, David Weigel expresses skepticism that this intervention will be effective. He points out that mainstream Republicans spent significant funds on ads to try to shore up the primary campaign of longtime senator Richard Lugar. Despite that, Lugar lost to Tea Party favorite Richard Mourdock—and Mourdock then went on to fumble the general election that Lugar just about certainly would have won. Weigel concludes that Republican primary voters are simply eager to elect pure conservatives who make extreme statements about culture-war issues, such as abortion or religion, which can backfire badly in general elections.

In the following chapter, commenters discuss other issues affecting Republican electoral chances, including demographic changes across the United States and voter ID laws.

> *"The dominant fact of the new Democratic majority is that it has begun to overturn the racial dynamics that have governed American politics for five decades."*

Republicans Face a Demographic Apocalypse

Jonathan Chait

Jonathan Chait is a writer for New York *magazine and a former editor at the* New Republic. *In the following viewpoint, he argues that demography is against the Republicans, who have become an aging white party, because the country is becoming increasingly diverse. Chait says that in 2012 the Republicans tried to win a final, resounding victory in their current form rather than adjusting to reach out to Hispanic and minority voters. He suggests that this decision will badly hurt the Republican Party in the long run.*

As you read, consider the following questions:

1. What was the argument of *The Emerging Democratic Majority?*

2. How does Chait believe the GOP has failed to reach out to Hispanic voters?

3. What does Chait believe Republicans could have done to sink health care reform?

Of the various expressions of right-wing hysteria that have flowered over the past three years—goldbuggery, birtherism, death panels at home and imaginary apology tours by President [Barack] Obama abroad[1]—perhaps the strain that has taken deepest root within mainstream Republican circles is the terror that the achievements of the Obama administration may be irreversible, and that the time remaining to stop permanent nightfall is dwindling away.

"Tipping Point"

"America is approaching a 'tipping point' beyond which the Nation will be unable to change course," announces the dark, old-timey preamble to [influential House member] Paul Ryan's "The Roadmap Plan," a statement of fiscal principles that shaped the budget outline approved last spring [in 2011] by 98 percent of the House Republican caucus. [Presidential candidate] Rick Santorum warns his audiences, "We are reaching a tipping point, folks, when those who pay are the minority and those who receive are the majority." Even such a sober figure as [Republican presidential candidate] Mitt Romney regularly says things like "We are only inches away from no longer being a free economy," and that this election "could be our last chance."

The Republican Party is in the grips of many fever dreams. But this is not one of them. To be sure, the apocalyptic *ideo-*

---

1. Goldbuggery refers to fears of inflation; birtherism is the claim that President Obama was not born in the United States and so is an illegitimate president; "death panels" refer to the fear that the health care law will result in government withholding health care and letting people die; apology tours refer to the claim that Obama apologizes for US history.

logical analysis—that "freedom" is incompatible with [Bill] Clinton–era tax rates and Massachusetts-style health care—is pure crazy. But the panicked *strategic* analysis, and the sense of urgency it gives rise to, is actually quite sound. The modern GOP [Grand Old Party, another name for the Republican Party]—the party of [Richard] Nixon, [Ronald] Reagan, and both [George H.W. and George W.] Bushes—is staring down its own demographic extinction. Right-wing warnings of impending tyranny express, in hyperbolic form, well-grounded dread: that conservative America will soon come to be dominated, in a semi-permanent fashion, by an ascendant Democratic coalition hostile to its outlook and interests. And this impending doom has colored the party's frantic, fearful response to the Obama presidency.

The GOP has reason to be scared. Obama's election was the vindication of a prediction made several years before by journalist John Judis and political scientist Ruy Teixeira in their 2002 book, *The Emerging Democratic Majority*. Despite the fact that George W. Bush then occupied the White House, Judis and Teixeira argued that demographic and political trends were converging in such a way as to form a natural-majority coalition for Democrats.

The Republican Party had increasingly found itself confined to white voters, especially those lacking a college degree and rural whites who, as Obama awkwardly put it in 2008, tend to "cling to guns or religion." Meanwhile, the Democrats had increased their standing among whites with graduate degrees, particularly the growing share of secular whites, and remained dominant among racial minorities. As a whole, Judis and Teixeira noted, the electorate was growing both somewhat better educated and dramatically less white, making every successive election less favorable for the GOP. And the trends were even more striking in some key swing states. Judis and Teixeira highlighted Colorado, Nevada, and Arizona, with skyrocketing Latino populations, and Virginia and North Carolina, with their influx of college-educated whites, as the most fertile grounds for the expanding Democratic base.

The Growing Wave

Obama's victory carried out the blueprint. Campaign reporters cast the election as a triumph of Obama's inspirational message and cutting-edge organization, but above all his sweeping win reflected simple demography. Every year, the nonwhite proportion of the electorate grows by about half a percentage point—meaning that in every presidential election, the minority share of the vote increases by 2 percent, a huge amount in a closely divided country. One measure of how thoroughly the electorate had changed by the time of Obama's election was that, if college-educated whites, working-class whites, and minorities had cast the same proportion of the votes in 1988 as they did in 2008, Michael Dukakis would have, just barely, won. By 2020—just eight years away—nonwhite voters should rise from a quarter of the 2008 electorate to one-third. In 30 years, nonwhites will outnumber whites.

Now, there are two points to keep in mind about the emerging Democratic majority. The first is that no coalition is permanent. One party can build a majority, but eventually the minority learns to adapt to an altered landscape, and parity returns. In 1969, Kevin Phillips, then an obscure Nixon-administration staffer, wrote *The Emerging Republican Majority*, arguing that Republicans could undo FDR's [Franklin Delano Roosevelt's] New Deal coalition by exploiting urban strife, the unpopularity of welfare, and the civil rights struggle to pull blue-collar whites into a new conservative bloc. The result was the modern GOP. Bill Clinton appropriated some elements of this conservative coalition by rehabilitating his party's image on welfare and crime (though he had a little help from Ross Perot, too). But it wasn't until Obama was elected that a Democratic president could claim to be the leader of a true majority party.

The second point is that short-term shocks, like war, recession, or scandal, can exert a far more powerful influence than a long-term trend: The Watergate scandal [that is, revelations of rampant criminalization in the Nixon administration], for instance, interrupted the Republican majority at its zenith, helping elect a huge raft of Democratic congressmen in 1974, followed two years later by Jimmy Carter.

But the dominant fact of the new Democratic majority is that it has begun to overturn the racial dynamics that have governed American politics for five decades. Whatever its abstract intellectual roots, conservatism has since at least the sixties drawn its political strength by appealing to heartland identity politics. In 1985, Stanley Greenberg, then a political scientist, immersed himself in Macomb County, a blue-collar Detroit suburb where whites had abandoned the Democratic Party in droves. He found that the Reagan Democrats there understood politics almost entirely in racial terms, translating any Democratic appeal to economic justice as taking their money to subsidize the black underclass. And it didn't end with the Reagan era. Piles of recent studies have found that voters often conflate "social" and "economic" issues. What social scientists delicately call "ethnocentrism" and "racial resentment" and "ingroup solidarity" are defining attributes of conservative voting behavior, and help organize a familiar if not necessarily rational coalition of ideological interests. Doctrines like neoconservative foreign policy, supply-side economics, and climate skepticism may bear little connection to each other at the level of abstract thought. But boiled down to political sound bites and served up to the voters, they blend into an indistinguishable stew of racial, religious, cultural, and nationalistic identity.

Obama's election dramatized the degree to which this long-standing political dynamic had been flipped on its head. In the aftermath of George McGovern's 1972 defeat, neoconservative intellectual Jeane Kirkpatrick disdainfully identified his voters as "intellectuals enamored with righteousness and possibility, college students, for whom perfectionism is an occupational hazard; portions of the upper classes freed from concern with economic self-interest," and so on, curiously neglecting to include racial minorities. All of them were, in essence, people who heard a term like "real American" and understood that in some way it did not apply to them. Today, cosmopolitan liberals may still feel like an embattled sect— they certainly describe their political fights in those terms— but time has transformed their rump minority into a collective majority. As conservative strategists will tell you, there are now more of "them" than "us." What's more, the disparity will continue to grow indefinitely. Obama actually lost the over-45-year-old vote in 2008, gaining his entire victory margin from younger voters—more racially diverse, better educated, less religious, and more socially and economically liberal.

Portents of this future were surely rendered all the more vivid by the startling reality that the man presiding over the new majority just happened to be, himself, young, urban, hip, and black. When jubilant supporters of Obama gathered in Grant Park on Election Night in 2008, Republicans saw a glimpse of their own political mortality. And a galvanizing picture of just what their new rulers would look like.

The Battle

In the cold calculus of game theory, the expected response to this state of affairs would be to accommodate yourself to the growing strength of the opposing coalition—to persuade pockets of voters on the Democratic margins they might be better served by Republicans. Yet the psychology of decline does not always operate in a straightforward, rational way. A strategy of managing slow decay is unpleasant, and history is replete with instances of leaders who persuaded themselves of the opposite of the obvious conclusion. Rather than adjust themselves to their slowly weakening position, they chose instead to stage a decisive confrontation. If the terms of the fight grow more unfavorable with every passing year, well, all the more reason to have the fight sooner. This was the thought process of the antebellum Southern states, sizing up the growing population and industrial might of the North. It was the thinking of the leaders of Austria-Hungary, watching their empire deteriorate and deciding they needed a decisive war [World War I] with Serbia to save themselves.

At varying levels of conscious and subconscious thought, this is also the reasoning that has driven Republicans in the Obama era. Surveying the landscape, they have concluded that they must strike quickly and decisively at the opposition before all hope is lost.

Arthur [C.] Brooks, the president of the conservative American Enterprise Institute and a high-profile presence on the Republican intellectual scene, wrote a 2010 book titled *The Battle*, urging conservatives to treat the struggle for economic libertarianism as a "culture war" between capitalism and socialism, in which compromise was impossible. Time was running short, Brooks pleaded in apocalyptic tones. The "real core" of what he called Obama's socialistic supporters was voters under 30. "It is the future of our country," he wrote. "And this group has exhibited a frightening openness to statism in the age of Obama."

The same panic courses through a new tome by James De-Mint, who has made himself probably the most influential member of the Senate by relentlessly pushing his colleagues to the right and organizing primary challenges to snuff out any hint of moderation among his co-partisans. DeMint's book, titled *Now or Never*, paints a haunting picture: "Republican supporters will continue to decrease every year as more Americans become dependent on the government. Dependent voters will naturally elect even big-government progressives who will continue to smother economic growth and spend America deeper into debt. The 2012 election may be the last opportunity for Republicans."

That apocalyptic rhetoric is just as common among voters as among conservative eggheads and party elites. Theda Skocpol, a Harvard sociologist, conducted a detailed study of Tea Party activists and discovered that they saw themselves beset by parasitic Democrats. "Along with illegal immigrants," she wrote, "low-income Americans and young people loom large as illegitimate consumers of public benefits and services."

It's easy for liberals to dismiss these fears as simple racism—and surely racism, to some degree, sways the Tea Party. But it is not just conservative white people who react fearfully when they see themselves outnumbered by an influx of people unlike themselves. Minorities do it. White hipsters do it. Recall the embarrassing spectacle of liberal panic, in the aftermath of George W. Bush's reelection, when [John] Kerry voters believed their country had been taken over by gay-bashing evangelical Christians.

That the struggles over the economic policies of the last few years have taken on the style of a culture war should come as no surprise, since conservatives believe Obama has pulled together an ascendant coalition of voters intent on expropriating their money. Paul Ryan, the House Republican budget chairman, has, like many Republicans, cast the fight as pitting "makers" against "takers," with the latter in danger of irrevocably gaining the upper hand. "The tipping point represents two dangers," he announced in a speech at the American Enterprise Institute, "first, long-term economic decline as the number of makers diminishes [and] the number of takers grows. . . . Second, gradual moral-political decline as dependency and passivity weaken the nation's character."

Resisting Immigration

Of course, both parties make use of end-times rhetoric, especially in election season. What's novel about the current spate of Republican millennialism is that it's not a mere rhetorical

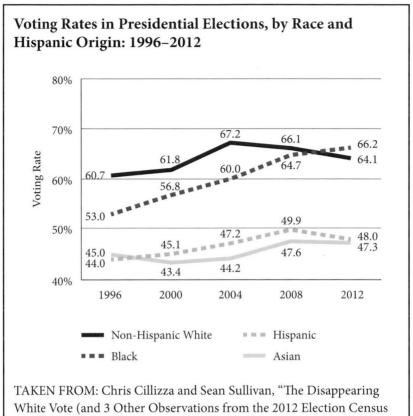

Voting Rates in Presidential Elections, by Race and Hispanic Origin: 1996–2012

TAKEN FROM: Chris Cillizza and Sean Sullivan, "The Disappearing White Vote (and 3 Other Observations from the 2012 Election Census Report)," *Washington Post*, May 10, 2013.

device to rally the faithful, nor even simply an expression of free-floating terror, but the premise of an electoral strategy.

In that light, the most surprising response to the election of 2008 is what did not happen. Following Obama's win, all sorts of loose talk concerning the Republican predicament filled the air. How would the party recast itself? Where would it move left, how would it find common ground with Obama, what new constituencies would it court?

The most widely agreed-upon component of any such undertaking was a concerted effort to win back the Hispanic vote. It seemed like a pure political no-brainer, a vital outreach to an exploding electoral segment that could conceivably be weaned from its Democratic leanings, as had previous generations of Irish and Italian immigrants, without altering the party's general right-wing thrust on other issues. George W. Bush had tried to cobble together a comprehensive immigration reform policy only to see it collapse underneath a conservative grassroots revolt, and [2008 presidential candidate] John McCain, who had initially cosponsored a bill in the Senate, had to withdraw his support for it in his pursuit of the 2008 nomination.

In the wake of his defeat, strategists like Karl Rove and Mike Murphy urged the GOP to abandon its stubborn opposition to reform. Instead, incredibly, the party adopted a more hawkish position, with Republicans in Congress rejecting even quarter-loaf compromises like the DREAM Act [referring to the Development, Relief, and Education for Alien Minors Act] and state-level officials like Jan Brewer launching new restrictionist crusades. This was, as Thomas Edsall writes in *The Age of Austerity*, "a major gamble that the GOP can continue to win as a white party despite the growing strength of the minority vote."

None of this is to say that Republicans ignored the rising tide of younger and browner voters that swamped them at the polls in 2008. Instead they set about keeping as many of them from the polls as possible. The bulk of the campaign has taken the form of throwing up an endless series of tedious bureaucratic impediments to voting in many states—ending same-day voter registration, imposing onerous requirements upon voter-registration drives, and upon voters themselves. "Voting liberal, that's what kids do," overshared William [Bill] O'Brien, the New Hampshire House speaker, who had supported a bill to prohibit college students from voting from their school addresses. What can these desperate, rearguard tactics accomplish? They can make the electorate a bit older, whiter, and less poor. They can, perhaps, buy the Republicans some time.

Obstruction as a Strategy

And to what end? The Republicans' most audacious choice is the hyperaggressive position they've adopted against Obama to sabotage his chances for a second term. Frustrated liberals, assessing the methods of the Republicans in Congress, see a devious brilliance at work in the GOP strategy of legislative obstruction. And indeed, Republicans very skillfully ground the legislative gears to a halt for months on end, weakening or killing large chunks of Obama's agenda, and nurturing public discontent with Washington that they rode to a sweeping victory in 2010. At the same time, their inability to waver from desperate, all-or-nothing opposition often meant conservatives willingly suffered policy defeats for perceived political gain, and failed to minimize the scale of those defeats.

Take the fight over health care reform. Yes, Republicans played the politics about as well as possible. But it was their hard line on compromise that allowed the bill to pass: The Democrats only managed to cobble together 60 votes to pass it in the Senate because conservatives drove Arlen Specter out of the GOP, forcing him to switch to the Democratic Party. Without him, Democrats never could have broken a filibuster. When Scott Brown surprisingly won the 2010 race to fill Ted Kennedy's Senate seat, Democrats were utterly despondent, and many proposed abandoning comprehensive health care reform to cut a deal for some meager expansion of children's health insurance. But Republicans refused to offer even an olive branch. Presented with a choice between passing the comprehensive bill they had spent a year cobbling together or collapsing in total ignominious defeat, the Democrats passed the bill.

Last summer, Obama was again desperate to reach compromise, this time on legislation to reduce the budget deficit, which had come to dominate the political agenda and symbolize, in the eyes of Establishment opinion, Obama's failure to fulfill his campaign goal of winning bipartisan cooperation. In extended closed-door negotiations, Obama offered Republicans hundreds of billions of dollars in spending cuts and a permanent extension of Bush-era tax rates in return for just $800 billion in higher revenue over a decade. This was less than half the new revenue proposed by the Bowles-Simpson deficit commission [referring to the National Commission on Fiscal Responsibility and Reform]. Republicans spurned this deal, too.

Instead the party has bet everything on 2012, preferring a Hail Mary strategy to the slow march of legislative progress. That is the basis of the House Republicans' otherwise inexplicable choice to vote last spring for a sweeping budget plan that would lock in low taxes, slash spending, and transform Medicare into private vouchers—none of which was popular with voters. Majority parties are known to hold unpopular votes occasionally, but holding an unpopular vote that Republicans knew full well stood zero chance of enactment (with Obama casting a certain veto) broke new ground in the realm of foolhardiness.

The way to make sense of that foolhardiness is that the party has decided to bet everything on its one "last chance." Not the last chance for the Republican Party to win power— there will be many of those, and over time it will surely learn to compete for nonwhite voters—but its last chance to exercise power in its current form, as a party of antigovernment fundamentalism powered by sublimated white Christian identity politics. (And the last chance to stop the policy steamroller of the new Democratic majority.) And whatever rhetorical concessions to moderates and independents the eventual Republican nominee may be tempted to make in the fall, he'll find himself fairly boxed in by everything he's already done this winter to please that base.

All or Nothing

Will the gamble work? Grim though the long-term demography may be, it became apparent to Republicans almost immediately after Obama took office that political fate had handed them an impossibly lucky opportunity. Democrats had come to power almost concurrently with the deepest economic crisis in 80 years, and Republicans quickly seized the tactical advantage, in an effort to leverage the crisis to rewrite their own political fortunes. The Lesser Depression could be an economic Watergate, the Republicans understood, an exogenous political shock that would, at least temporarily, overwhelm any deeper trend, and possibly afford the party a chance to permanently associate the Democrats with the painful aftermath of the crisis.

During the last midterm elections, the strategy succeeded brilliantly. Republicans moved further right and won a gigantic victory. In the 2010 electorate, the proportion of voters under 30 fell by roughly a third, while the proportion of voters over 65 years old rose by a similar amount—the white share, too. In the long run, though, the GOP has done nothing at all to rehabilitate its deep unpopularity with the public as a whole, and has only further poisoned its standing with Hispanics. But by forswearing compromise, it opened the door to a single shot. The Republicans have gained the House and stand poised to win control of the Senate. If they can claw out a presidential win and hold on to Congress, they will have a glorious two-year window to restore the America they knew and loved, to lock in transformational change, or at least to wrench the status quo so far rightward that it will take Democrats a generation to wrench it back. The cost of any foregone legislative compromises on health care or the deficit would be trivial compared to the enormous gains available to a party in control of all three federal branches.

On the other hand, if they lose their bid to unseat Obama, they will have mortgaged their future for nothing at all. And over the last several months, it has appeared increasingly likely that the party's great all-or-nothing bet may land, ultimately, on nothing. In which case, the Republicans will have turned an unfavorable outlook into a truly bleak one in a fit of panic. The deepest effect of Obama's election upon the Republicans' psyche has been to make them truly fear, for the first time since before Ronald Reagan, that the future is against them.

> *"No one has yet proved that the 2012 election indicates that the Republican Party needs to change fundamentally in order to win."*

Republicans Do Not Face a Demographic Apocalypse

Harry J. Enten

Harry J. Enten is senior political writer at FiveThirtyEight *and also has written for the* Guardian. *In the following viewpoint, he argues that in the 2012 presidential election Republicans did about as well as could be expected given the economy at the time. Based on this, he argues that Republicans face no inevitable demographic decline. He says that while Republicans have been losing among minority voters, they have gained more and more support among white voters, putting them in a position to win in 2016 and later if the economy is poor or the electorate is generally dissatisfied.*

As you read, consider the following questions:

1. What does Enten say almost always determines election results?

2. Among what group is Barack Obama's support weakest and dropping, according to Enten?

3. With what coalition does Enten think the Republicans could win the 2016 election?

The fault line in the GOP [Grand Old Party, another name for the Republican Party] revealed by the party's internal debate on immigration reform—over whether a future Republican coalition should rely more heavily on whites than it already does, or should try and bring more Latinos into the fold to win the presidency—remains unresolved. What we can say is that the last election and current polling suggest that the Republicans' path of least resistance is to win even more non-college-educated whites and to try to win somewhat more of the minority vote.

Romney Did Fine

Start with the fact that in 2012 [Barack] Obama lost a little more than 3pt off his margin of victory in 2008. That swing was not uniform. It's fairly clear that Obama's share fell significantly with white voters without a college education, stayed about level with whites with a college degree, gained a few points with Latinos, and may have lost a point or two with black voters.

I don't view the incongruity between those shifts as a sign that Obama should have done worse or better. In any election, you're given a certain amount of leverage by the state of the economy, and you need to use it where you can. In 2012, the parties found the coalitions that worked for them. It just so happened that Obama had more room for growth electorally because the economy was "good enough".

Indeed, there is little to no sign that [Republican presidential candidate] Mitt Romney did worse than he should have, given the state of the economy. President Obama won by a little less than 4pt, when the two best fundamental models

White Voters for Obama

Although minority voters were critical to [Barack] Obama's presidential victory in 2008, he would not have won without the support of white Americans who made up the largest ethnic group in the election. According to NBC News director Chuck Todd and elections director Sheldon Gawiser, "Obama ran as well with white voters nationwide as any previous Democratic candidate since Jimmy Carter in 1976; Carter garnered 47 percent of the white vote. In 2008, Obama tallied 43 percent of the white vote nationwide as compared to John McCain's 55 percent of the white vote." Obama fared better among white voters than recent Democratic candidates. For example, John Kerry, the Democratic Party nominee in 2004, received 41 percent of the white vote, two percentage points less than Obama received in 2008. This was an amazing percentage given all the hype about racism still being very prevalent and how America (white America in particular) was not ready to elect a black American as president.

The majority of whites, however, continued to vote Republican. Strong opposition to Obama was limited to several demographic groups. While much of the opposition came from the white working class.

Dewey M. Clayton,
The Presidential Campaign of Barack Obama:
A Critical Analysis of a Racially Transcendent Strategy.
New York: Routledge, 2010, p. 70.

(based solely on numerous different economic factors) had him winning by 3pt and 5pt respectively. Taking into account Obama's approval rating *and* the economy, as the original Alan Abramowitz model does, shows Obama should have won by a little more than 4pt.

That's the reason why I don't buy the argument that the shrinking white population in this country necessarily spells doom for the Republicans. This is a two-party system where the economy almost always dictates who wins and loses elections. No one has yet proved that the 2012 election indicates that the Republican Party needs to change fundamentally in order to win, despite hundreds of column inches expended on the subject.

For Republicans to win, they'd need economic conditions slightly more favorable to the out-party (that would have been, in 2012, a worse economy and less confidence). Following the 2012 pattern, this would allow them in 2016 to continue to do exponentially better among white working-class voters. Sean Trende, who believes that the GOP could win with a mostly white coalition, anticipates Republicans also gaining a few more points among minorities.

Of course, many doubt this steady-state strategy could work for Republicans. Karl Rove said a few months ago that Republicans would have a hard time regularly winning the white vote by 25pt or more. But that's the funny thing about electoral rules: they're made to be broken. For example, the aforementioned Alan Abramowitz said that Republicans would have a very hard time getting above the 58% of the white vote in 2010 that they had in 1994. In fact, they won 62% of the white vote in the last midterms.

That's why Trende has vigorously argued that the demographic wall facing the GOP doesn't really exist. The worsening Democratic performance among white voters we have seen recently is part of a long-standing trend. If the pattern continues, then white support for Democrats will continue to drop below its current historic low.

Democrats and White Voters

So, now we have a test case of sorts in 2014. The economy really hasn't gone south. Economic confidence is far higher than it was at the beginning of 2013, although it has stalled slightly. The percentage of those who view economic recovery as imminent has fallen slightly over the past few months, but it's only slightly lower than where it was at the time of the 2012 election. Put another way, there hasn't been that level of decline in the economy which many thought would need to happen for Republicans to win with the coalition they have.

Yet, Obama's net approval rating with white voters is no better than -25pt right now. His approval in Gallup's polling among white voters since the NSA [National Security Agency] leaks is now only 34.5%. That's a 4.5pt drop since the election. Pew [Research Center] has it slightly lower, at 33%, which is a 6pt drop off what Obama was showing in their final pre-election poll last year. It seems as though that wall keeps moving.

Most, if not all, of this drop for Obama is among whites without a college degree. Pew found support from that segment of the electorate dropping by a little less than 10pt. In other words, there is a continuity here with the November election result, in which Obama's support fell the furthest among whites without a college degree. If you think this might be pegged to public reaction to the Trayvon Martin case, the [George] Zimmerman verdict and the president's response,[1] it's not. Pew found college-educated whites reacted in the same way as non-college-educated whites to that issue—yet Obama has seen no decline in his standing among college-educated white voters.

Indeed, the swing looks much as expected: We have that drop among the non-college-educated whites, and among minorities to a smaller degree. We can see this by pooling Gallup's data since the Edward Snowden/NSA affair[2]; this gives us a very large sample size. That's important because mi-

---

1. George Zimmerman shot Trayvon Martin, an unarmed black teen, in 2012 in Florida. Martin died; Zimmerman was acquitted.
2. Snowden leaked information about government spying.

nority sample size in polls is often very small, which is why Pew and NBC News/*Wall Street Journal* differed so much in their minority findings this week. Gallup splits the difference and discovers that non-white approval of Obama has fallen since the election by 4pt, or about half of the drop we've seen with non-college-educated whites.

Republicans Have a Chance

Now, things could change and this analysis may end up way out of date come 2016. I should also add that the eventual party coalitions may look somewhat different then, with Republicans winning back some African-American voters once Obama is out of office, but maybe also Democrats making a slight recovery with white voters.

But the most salient fact is that Obama's approval among registered voters is a weak 45%—and that's without a bad dip in the economy or any grave scandal. This soft approval rating gives credence to what the polling suggests: that the Republican Party is most likely to win the White House in 2016 with a coalition that includes even more non-college-educated whites and a slight increase among minority voters.

"I doubt that most Republican voters know that some Republican officials are taking steps to make it even harder to get that ID."

Republicans Push Voter ID Laws to Disenfranchise Democratic Constituencies

Jeremiah Goulka

Jeremiah Goulka writes for TomDipatch.com, the American Prospect, and Salon; he was formerly an analyst at the RAND Corporation. In the following viewpoint, he argues that voter identification (ID) laws disproportionately affect the poor and minorities, who often don't have forms of identification and find it difficult to obtain them. He says that most Republican voters don't realize how voter ID laws disproportionately damage Democratic constituents. However, he suggests that Republican politicians are aware that voter ID laws hurt Democratic voters and promote such laws for partisan reasons.

As you read, consider the following questions:

1. According to Goulka, what about his own personal experiences makes him well positioned to explain why Republicans support voter ID laws?

2. What has Scott Walker done that suggests that voter ID laws in Wisconsin are intended to benefit Republicans?

3. What policies does Goulka suggest to make getting an ID less onerous?

Democrats are frustrated: Why can't Republican voters see that Republicans pass voter ID [identification] laws to suppress voting, not fraud?

Democrats know who tends to lack ID. They know that the threat of in-person voter fraud is wildly exaggerated. Besides, Republican officials could hardly have been clearer about the real purpose behind these laws and courts keep striking them down as unconstitutional. Still, Republican support remains sky-high, with only one-third of Republicans recognizing that they are primarily intended to boost the GOP's [the Grand Old Party, another name for the Republican Party] prospects.

How can Republican voters go on believing that the latest wave of voter ID laws is about fraud and that it's the *opposition* to the laws that's being partisan?

To help frustrated non-Republicans, I offer up my own experience as a case study. I was a Republican for most of my life, and during those years I had no doubt that such laws were indeed truly about fraud. Please join me on a tour of my old outlook on voter ID laws and what caused it to change.

Fraud on the Brain

I grew up in a wealthy Republican suburb of Chicago, where we worried about election fraud all the time. Showing our IDs at the polls seemed like a minor act of political rebellion against the legendary Democratic political machine that ran the city and county. "Vote early and often!" was the catchphrase we used for how that machine worked. Those were its instructions to its minions, we semi-jokingly believed, and it called up an image of mass in-person voter fraud.

We hated the "Democrat" machine, seeing it as inherently corrupt, and its power, we had no doubt, derived from fraud. When it wasn't bribing voters or destroying ballots, it was manipulating election laws—creating, for instance, a signature-collecting requirement so onerous that only a massive organization like itself could easily gather enough John Hancocks to put its candidates on the ballot.

Republicans with long memories still wonder if Richard Nixon lost Illinois—and the 1960 election—thanks to Chicago mayor Richard Daley's ability to make dead Republicans vote for John F. Kennedy. For us, any new report of voter fraud, wrapped in rumor and historical memory, just hammered home what we already knew: It was rampant in our county thanks to the machine.

And it wasn't just Chicago. We assumed that all cities were run by similarly corrupt Democratic organizations. As for stories of rural corruption and vote tampering? You can guess which party we blamed. Corruption, election fraud, and Democrats: They went hand-in-hand-in-hand.

Sure, we were aware of the occasional accusation of corruption against one or another Republican official. Normally, we assumed that such accusations were politically motivated. If they turned out to be true, then you were obviously talking about a "bad apple."

I must admit that I did occasionally wonder whether there were any Republican machines out there, and the more I heard about the dominating one in neighboring DuPage County, the less I wanted to know. Still, I knew—I *knew*—that the Dems would use any crooked tool in the box to steal elections. Therefore, America needed cleaner elections, and cleaner elections meant voter ID laws.

Doesn't Everyone Have an ID?

Every once in a while I'd hear the complaint—usually from a Democrat—that such laws were "racist." Racist? How could they be when they were so commonsensical? The complainers, I figured, were talking nonsense, just another instance of the tiresome PC [politically correct] brigade slapping the race card on the table for partisan advantage. If only they would scrap their tedious, tendentious identity and victim politics and come join the rest of us in the business of America.

All this held until one night in 2006. At the time, my roommate worked at a local bank branch, and that evening when we got into a conversation, he mentioned to me that the bank required two forms of identification to open an account. Of course, who wouldn't? But then he told me this crazy thing: Customers would show up with only one ID or none at all—and it wasn't like they had left them at home.

"Really?" I said, blown away by the thought of it.

"Yeah, really."

And here was the kicker: Every single one of them was black and poor. As I've written elsewhere, this was one of the moments that opened my eyes to a broader reality which, in the end, caused me to quit the Republican Party.

I had no idea. I had naturally assumed—to the extent that I even gave it a thought—that every adult had to have at least one ID. Like most everyone in my world, I've had two or three at any given time since the day I turned 16 and begged my parents to take me to the DMV [Department of Motor Vehicles].

Until then, I couldn't imagine how voter ID laws might be about anything but fraud. That no longer held up for the simple reason that, in the minds of Republican operators and voters alike, there is a pretty simple equation: Black + Poor = Democrat. And if that was the case, and the poor and black were more likely to lack IDs, then how could those laws *not* be aimed at them?

Whenever I tell people this story, most Republicans and some Democrats are shocked. Like me, they had no idea that there are significant numbers of adults out there who don't have IDs.

Of course, had I bothered to look, the information about this was hiding in plain sight. According to the respected Brennan Center for Justice at the New York University School of Law, 7% of the general voting public doesn't have an adequate photo ID, but those figures rise precipitously when you hit certain groups: 15% of voting age citizens making less than $35,000 a year, 18% of Americans over 65, and a full quarter of African Americans.

A recent study by other researchers focusing on the swing state of Pennsylvania found that one in seven voters there lack an ID—one in three in Philadelphia—with minorities far more likely than whites to fall into this category. In fact, every study around notes this disparate demographic trend, even the low-number outlier study preferred by Hans van Spakovsky, the conservative Heritage Foundation's voter "integrity" activist: Its authors still found that "registered voters without photo IDs tended to be female, African-American, and Democrat."

The "R" Bomb

The more I thought about it, the more I understood why Democrats claim that these laws are racist. By definition, a law that intentionally imposes more burdens on minorities than on whites is racist, even if that imposition is indirect. Seeing these laws as distant relatives of literacy tests and poll taxes no longer seemed so outrageous to me.

After I became a Democrat, I tried explaining this to some of the Republicans in my life, but I quickly saw that I had crossed an invisible trip wire. You see, if you ever want to get a Republican to stop listening to you, just say the "R" word: racism. In my Republican days, any time a Democrat started talking about how some Republican policy or act was racist, I

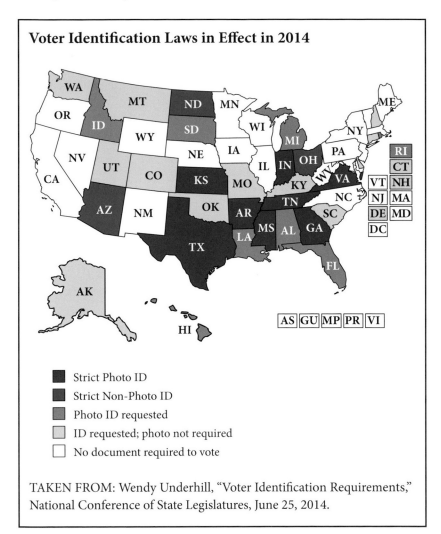

Voter Identification Laws in Effect in 2014

Legend:
- Strict Photo ID
- Strict Non-Photo ID
- Photo ID requested
- ID requested; photo not required
- No document required to vote

TAKEN FROM: Wendy Underhill, "Voter Identification Requirements," National Conference of State Legislatures, June 25, 2014.

rolled my eyes and thought Reaganesquely [that is, pertaining to former Republican president Ronald Reagan], *there they go again. . . .*

We loathed identity politics, which we viewed as invidious—as well as harmful to minorities. And the "race card" was so simplistic, so partisan, so boring. Besides, what about all that reverse discrimination? Now *that* was racist.

We also hated any accusation that made it sound like we were personally racist. It's a big insult to call someone a racist

or a bigot, and we loathed it when Democrats associated the rest of us Republicans with the bigots in the party. At least in my world, we rejected racism, which we defined (in what I now see as a conveniently narrow way) as intentional and mean-spirited acts or attitudes—like the laws passed by segregationist *Democrats.*

This will undoubtedly amaze non-Republicans, but given all of the above, Republican voters continue to hear the many remarkably blunt statements by those leading the Republican drive to pass voter ID laws not as racist but at the very worst *Democratist.* That includes comments like that of Pennsylvania House majority leader Mike Turzai who spoke of "voter ID, which is going to allow Governor Romney to win the state of Pennsylvania: done." Or state Representative Alan Clemmons, the principal sponsor of South Carolina's voter ID law, who handed out bags of peanuts with this note attached: "Stop Obama's nutty agenda and support voter ID."

Besides, some would point out that these laws also affect other people like the elderly (who often vote Republican) or out-of-state college students (often white)—and the latter would make sense as a target, because in the words of New Hampshire House leader Bill O'Brien, that's the age when you tend to "foolishly . . . do what kids do": "vote as a liberal." And yes, this might technically violate the general principle that clean elections should include everyone, but partisans won't mind the results.

This makes me wonder how bothered I would have been had I known how committed Republican strategists are to winning elections by shrinking the electorate rather than appealing to more of it. I did certainly harbor a quiet suspicion that, to the extent we were the party of the managerial class, we were inherently fated to be a minority party.

The Safety Valve

Another key reason why Republican voters see no problem with these laws is their big safety valve: If you don't have an ID, well, then, be responsible and go get one!

If, however, Republican voters are generally unaware of the high frequency of minorities, the poor, and the elderly lacking IDs, they are blissfully ignorant of the real costs of getting an ID. Yes, the ID itself is free for the indigent (to comport with the 24th Amendment's ban on poll taxes), but the documents one needs to get a photo ID aren't, and the prices haven't been reduced. Lost your naturalization certificate? That'll be $345. Don't have a birth certificate because you're black and were born in the segregated south? You have to go to court.

Similarly, Republican voters—and perhaps most others—tend not to be aware of how hard it can be to get an ID if you live in a state where DMV offices are far away or where they simply aren't open very often. One can only hope that would-be voters have access to a car or adequate public transportation, and a boss who won't mind if they take several hours off work to go get their ID, particularly if they live in, say, the third of Texas counties that have no ID-issuing offices at all.

I doubt that most Republican voters know that some Republican officials are taking steps to make it even harder to get that ID. Wisconsin governor Scott Walker, to take an example, signed a strict voter ID law and then made a move to start closing DMV offices in areas full of Democrats, while increasing office hours in areas full of Republicans—this in a state in which half of blacks and Hispanics are estimated to lack a driver's license and a quarter of its DMV offices are open less than one day per month. (Sauk City's is open a whopping four times a year.) Somehow I doubt that this is primarily about saving money.

One reason why voter ID laws are so politically successful is that they put Democrats in a weak position, forcing them to deny that in-person voter fraud exists or that it's a big deal. Republican voters and media simply won't buy that. It doesn't matter how many times the evidence of the so-called threat has been shown to be trumped up. It's a bad position to be in.

oviding examples of Republicans committing fraud
nselves—whether in-person or, as in Massachusetts and
orida, with absentee ballots (a category curiously exempted
from several of the Republican-inspired voter ID statutes)—
won't provide a wake-up call either. Most Republican voters
will shrug it off by saying, essentially, "everybody's doing it."

If we can't talk about race, and Republican voters insist
that these laws really are about fraud, then maybe Democrats
should consider a different tack and embrace them to the
full—so long as they are redesigned to do no harm. IDs would
have to be truly free and easy to obtain. The poor should not
be charged for the required documentation. More DMVs
should be opened, particularly in poor neighborhoods and rural areas, and all DMVs should have evening and weekend
hours so that no one has to miss work to get an ID.

To be sure that the laws do no harm, how about mobile
DMV units that could go straight to any area where people
need IDs? Nursing homes, churches, senior centers, you name
it. They could even register people to vote at the same time.
Now that would be efficient—and democratic.

No, wait, I've got it: How about a mandatory ID card? Every American would receive a photo ID as soon as he or she
turns 18. That's it! A national ID card!

Then voter ID laws would be the perfect thing, because we
all want clean elections with high voter turnout, don't we?

Something tells me, though, that Republicans won't go for
it.

"Flagrant disregard of voter ID require-
ments has the potential to become a
political flash point."

Countering the Attack on Voter ID Laws

James Walsh

James Walsh is a writer for Newsweek. *In the following view-*
point, he argues that there is a failure on the nation's part to en-
force immigration laws. According to the author, this has, in
turn, given rise to the movement of providing non-citizens with
the right to vote. The author explains that voter identification
(ID) laws are meant to protect against voter fraud from such
movements. He suggests that Democratic priorities are clearly
partisan, and he concludes that more of a focus on voter fraud is
needed.

As you read, consider the following questions:

1. According to Walsh, what does the move to give non-citizens the right to vote reflect?

2. According to the viewpoint, how many states does the National Conference of State Legislatures list as having voter identification laws?

3. Why are voter identification laws necessary, according to the author?

Civil and ethnic rights organizations, with the support of the Obama administration, are intent on disrupting voting this November.

Their modus operandi is widespread filing of lawsuits that attack state voter identification laws. These lawsuits have been filed in a number of states under the guise of protecting minorities, the poor, and the elderly.

When state laws protecting the sanctity of the voting system are weakened or overturned, then voting anarchy results. For example, radical groups are seeking to overturn state laws that prevent non-citizens from voting. Although the Constitution leaves it to the states to determine qualifications for state voting, a federal law passed in 1996 makes it a crime for non-citizens to vote in federal elections (Title 18 USC section 611).

The current move to give non-citizens the right to vote in state and federal elections reflects the failure of the nation to enforce existing immigration laws. Immigration anarchy and non-citizen voting result from the lawlessness that follows when a nation abdicates control of its borders.

The *Washington Post*, on September 23, 2012, headlined a story, "Laws may cut Latino Voting—Rules could deter 10 million—Backers deny racism, say fraud is target." The newspaper based its story on a report by the Advancement Project (Ad.P), whose website slogan reads, "We are all immigrants." The group, founded in 1999 to forge a broad national immigrant rights movement, consists of aging leftist lawyers and social justice ingénues.

The Ad.P report decries the potential impact of newly restrictive photo identification laws, proof-of-citizenship requirements, and efforts by states to remove non-citizens from voter rolls. The group's concern that non-citizens might be prohibited from voting is based on the misinformed belief that non-citizens have the right to vote in U.S. elections.

Back in 2009, when the Democrats held the White House and majorities in both chambers of Congress—the U.S. Senate and the House of Representatives—President Obama could have passed an immigration reform bill but chose not to. In 2012, the president again promised Hispanics that, in his second term, he would push for immigration reform legislation.

Recently, when reporters on the Hispanic TV network Univisión, surprised Obama with hard questions regarding his tenure as president, he dodged the questions with vacuous responses. Not surprisingly, he proceeded to blame Republicans for his failures in immigration reform. It was obvious, however, that the reporters and audience did not buy his excuses.

Because of Obama's failures on immigration reform, including voter protection, many states took up the gauntlet to protect the right of citizens to vote. The National Conference of State Legislatures (NCSL) lists 33 states with voter identification (ID) laws as well as those state legislatures that are strengthening their voter ID laws.

When it comes to voter ID, not all states are equal. According to Section 5 of the Voting Rights Act of 1965, as part of the Democrats' War on Poverty, certain counties and cities across the United States must receive "pre-clearance" from the U.S. Department of Justice (DOJ) before enacting voting requirements.

A number of states are contesting the demands of the Obama Justice Department with regard to voter ID legislation. On voter ID, all states should be equal.

In 2008, the U.S. Supreme Court upheld Indiana's voter ID law. Justice John Paul Stevens, considered a liberal, wrote for the majority that the risk of voter fraud was real, even if no cases of voter fraud were established and that each state has the obligation to assure that only the votes of eligible voters are counted. Obama has chosen to ignore this decision.

In 2011, Rhode Island, which has a Democrat-controlled state Senate and House, passed a voter ID law. The U.S. Department of Justice (DOJ) chose not to file an objection to the law, thus disregarding claims by the American Civil Liberties Union (ACLU), National Association for the Advancement of Colored People (NAACP), and other leftist groups that it was discriminatory to minorities, the poor, and the elderly.

To date, courts have found that states challenged on their voter protection laws have valid, constitutional grounds. Some laws, however, have been overturned because of short notice times. For example, on Oct. 2, 2012, in Pennsylvania, where 59 percent of registered voters favor the requirement of photo IDs to vote, a state judge ruled that the state's voter ID law was void for the 2012 election but would be valid thereafter.

The voter ID law is either valid or it is not. Might politics have played a role in this "Alice in Wonderland" decision?

Voter ID laws are necessary to protect legitimate voting from voter fraud, such as the temporary movement of noncitizens from a "safe" state to a neighboring "swing" state to vote. Flagrant disregard of voter ID requirements has the potential to become a political flash point.

The nation depends on strong states that, empowered by the Constitution, pass and enforce voter ID requirements.

Periodical and Internet Sources Bibliography

The following articles have been selected to supplement the diverse views presented in this chapter.

Amy E. Black	"GOP Isn't Dying, but It Will Have to Reach Moderate Voters to Survive," *Christian Science Monitor*, August 19, 2013.
Eric Boehlert	"This Is How Fox News 'Saved' the GOP?," *Media Matters for America* (blog), April 29, 2014.
Philip Bump	"Democrats Are in Trouble in North Carolina, Everywhere Else Thanks to Demographics," The Wire, April 28, 2014.
Don Campbell	"Republicans Need to Become a More Diverse Party," *USA Today*, June 22, 2011.
Chris Cillizza	"The South Is Solidly Republican Right Now. It Might Not Be That Way in 10 Years," *Washington Post*, April 29, 2014.
Dave Jamieson	"Colin Powell: Voter ID Laws Will 'Backfire' for Republicans," *Huffington Post*, August 25, 2013.
Ian Millhiser	"GOP Official Resigns After Saying Purpose of Voter ID Is to Suppress Votes of Democrats, 'Lazy Blacks,'" *ThinkProgress*, October 25, 2013.
Alex Roarty	"Can Republicans Avoid the Next Todd Akin?," *National Journal*, September 26, 2013.
Reihan Salam and Rich Lowry	"The Party of Work: It Was Once the Republicans, and It Should Be Again," *National Review Online*, March 17, 2014.
David Weigel	"How to Stop the Next Todd Akin," *Slate*, February 4, 2013.

OPPOSING
VIEWPOINTS®
SERIES

CHAPTER 2

What Is the Relationship of Republicans to Important Voting Groups?

Chapter Preface

In the past, Asian Americans often have voted for Republican candidates. Leon Hadar in a November 9, 2012, article for *American Conservative* points out that many Asian Americans after 1945 were refugees from Communist regimes such as China, North Korea, and Vietnam and that they "tended to identify with the conservative and anti-Communist agenda of the Republican Party." Republican president Ronald Reagan won a majority of the Asian American vote in 1980 and 1984. Republican George H.W. Bush received 55 percent of the Asian American vote, compared to Bill Clinton's 31 percent, though Clinton won the election overall.

More recently, though, Republicans have begun to lose Asian American votes by substantial margins. According to Lloyd Green in a February 26, 2013, article at the Daily Beast website, Democrat Barack Obama won 62 percent of the Asian American vote in 2008 and a whopping 73 percent in 2012.

So why this shift from Republican support to Democratic? Hadar and Green suggest that part of the problem is that younger Asians often are well educated, and many pursue careers in technical fields. Republicans have had problems appealing to college graduates in tech fields, perhaps in part because the party's discomfort with the science of evolution and climate change makes it appear anti-education and anti-science. Republican hostility to immigration that hurts the party with Hispanics also damages it with Asian Americans. Hadar adds that "the obsession of so many Republicans and conservatives with birtherism [the suggestion that President Barack Obama was not born in the United States and is therefore an illegitimate president] and with the president's alleged Muslim faith only helps to accentuate the notion that Republicans are hostile toward immigrants and toward Americans who are non-white and non-Christian."

Republicans are working to regain ground among Asian American voters, according to Josie Huang in a February 10, 2014, article at 89.3 KPCC. Huang reports that the Republican National Committee (RNC) has hired staff in California and Washington, DC, to focus explicitly on Asian American issues. "Rather than swooping into town months before an election," Huang says, "the RNC's strategy is to develop a long-standing presence where Asian-Americans live, work and worship." Huang also notes that Republicans feel that their message of "lower taxes, quality education, public safety" can resonate with many Asian Americans.

The authors of the viewpoints in the following chapter examine the Republican Party's relationship with other important demographic groups, including Hispanics, women, and evangelicals.

> "There's the scary possibility that Florida goes the way of Nevada: the next Democrat would win Florida by 9 points if they merely did as well as [John] Kerry among Florida's white voters."

The Swing State Where the GOP Desperately Needs Hispanics

Nate Cohn

Nate Cohn is a journalist focusing on election coverage and polling for the New York Times *and formerly for the* New Republic. *In the following viewpoint, he argues that Florida's demographics are shifting as more Hispanics move into the state. He says that Republicans, who do not do well with non-Cuban Hispanic voters, will find it difficult to win Florida as this trend continues. Cohn contends that since Florida is an important state with many electoral votes, the changing demographics may seriously affect Republican chances of winning presidential elections if they do not find some way to appeal to Hispanic voters.*

As you read, consider the following questions:

1. In what states does Cohn say demographic changes have already shifted from Republican to Democrat?

2. Why doesn't Cohn think Republicans can perpetually run up the vote total among white voters?

3. What are the demographics of black voters in Florida, and does this help or hurt the GOP (Grand Old Party, another name for the Republican Party), according to Cohn?

Opponents of immigration reform are right about one thing: Hispanics aren't enough for Republicans to win back the White House. But that doesn't mean that the GOP can sacrifice Hispanics without big consequences for their chances. That's already happened in New Mexico and Nevada, where the Hispanic vote has flipped two states from red to blue. The GOP's route to the presidency has survived the loss of those two small states—they're worth just 11 electoral votes. But it's a whole different story if Florida suffers the same fate as Nevada, as it very well might if Republicans can't improve among Hispanics.

Florida's Hispanic population has exploded over the last decade, growing by 57 percent between 2000 and 2010. As a result, the Hispanic share of eligible voters surged from 12.5 percent to 16.8 percent between 2004 and 2012, while non-Hispanic whites dropped from 72.2 to 65.8 percent. Those new Hispanic voters aren't Republican-leaning Cubans, either. They're a mix of heavily Democratic Puerto Ricans who surged to Orlando-Kissimmee and a mix of Hispanics from elsewhere in Central and South America. As a result, Cubans now represent just 32 percent of Florida's voting eligible Hispanics. The new Cuban voters aren't as Republican, either: Younger third generation Cubans have little memory of the Cold War and don't associate Democrats with Soviets, like their parents and grandparents.

The combination of Democratic gains among Hispanics nationally and an influx of more Democratic-friendly Hispanics has flipped the state's Hispanic vote. In 2004, Florida's Latinos voted for [George W.] Bush by 12 points, 56–44. Just eight years later, [Barack] Obama won Latinos by a decisive 21 points, 60–39. This huge shift has upended Florida's well-known political geography. Orange and Osceola Counties, home to Orlando and Kissimmee, were once the country's premier swing counties at the heart of the country's premier swing region, the I-4 corridor. They voted for Bush by just .07 percent and 3669 votes in 2004. But in 2012, Obama won these two counties by a massive 19 point and 111,723 vote margin. Miami-Dade County used to only lean slightly toward Democrats: it voted for [John] Kerry by 6 points, or 48,637 votes. Now it's a rout for Democrats. In 2012, Obama won by 24 points and 208,459 votes.

Despite these extremely favorable trends, Obama still only won Florida by less than 1 percent or 74,000 votes. That might seem to make Florida the perfect candidate for the GOP to win with additional gains among white voters—they wouldn't need to do so much better to win, just one more point. But the "more whites" strategy might not work in Florida.

Florida was so close because the GOP has already made huge gains among white voters—bigger than any other battleground state. Obama lost Florida's whites by 24 points, 10 points worse than Kerry's more modest, 14 point defeat in 2004. The following map [not included] shows where Obama performed better or worse than Kerry. In the red areas (yes this is a counter-intuitive color scheme), like the diversifying I-4 corridor and Miami, Obama did much better than Kerry. The blue areas, like the panhandle or the retirement communities along the Gold Coast, are where Kerry did better than Obama.

There's a long list of reasons why Obama was a bad fit for Florida's whites; a worse fit than other Democrats. Obama did not perform well among culturally Southern whites, including in northern and central Florida. Obama was weak among white seniors, who represent 28 percent of Florida's eligible white voters, and probably an even larger share of the electorate. At the same time, the departure of the heavily Democratic "Greatest Generation" probably hurt Obama among whites—seniors voted for Bush by just 3 or 4 points against Kerry and [Al] Gore. Obama always seemed to do best among young, well-educated white voters in post-industrial metropolitan areas—Raleigh, Denver-Boulder, or northern Virginia—but there are few similar areas in the Sunshine State. If Democrats have a base among Florida's whites, it's the state's heavily Democratic Jewish population. But that was never one of the president's strengths, either.

That raises the possibility that Republicans are close to maximizing their share of the white vote in Florida. Certainly, they're closer to maximizing it in Florida than they are in other states, like Colorado or Wisconsin, where Obama seemed to have appeal and where Republicans have done better in recent memory. It seems quite possible that the Democrats could nominate a candidate who stems the bleeding, or even does better among Florida's whites. It's worth noting that Bill Nelson and Alex Sink both did much better among white voters than Obama did last November. Early polls show Hillary Clinton crushing in Florida by a double-digit margin because she's doing far better among whites than Obama—about as well as Gore. Those tallies would have been a dead heat a decade ago, but now result in a comfortable Democratic win.

Even if Democrats did nominate another poor fit, it's not a state where Republicans can expect to perpetually run up the score among white voters. Florida is not Alabama. It's a diverse state with a white population that's vaguely representative of the country, and therefore includes plenty of Democratic-leaning moderates or even liberals. Twenty-five percent of the state's white voters were Jewish or non-

Active Registered Voters in Florida, by Race and Ethnicity, 2006 to 2012 (in thousands)

	Hispanic		White		Black		Asian		Total	
	#	%	#	%	#	%	#	%	#	%
2012	1,660	13.9	7,939	66.5	1,620	13.6	194	1.6	11,934	100.0
2010	1,426	12.7	7,693	68.6	1,460	13.0	165	1.5	11,217	100.0
2008	1,355	12.0	7,773	69.1	1,469	13.1	151	1.3	11,248	100.0
2006	1,114	10.7	7,509	72.0	1,248	12.0	120	1.1	10,434	100.0

Notes: Data represent registration as of book-closing dates. "Asian" includes Pacific Islanders. Percentages calculated before rounding. Total includes some groups not shown separately (e.g., Native Americans).

Source: Florida Department of State Division of Elections.

http://election.dos.state.fl.us/voter-registration/statistics/elections.shtml

Pew Research Center

TAKEN FROM: Seth Motel and Eileen Patten, "Latinos in the 2012 Election: Florida," Pew Research Center, November 5, 2012.

Christian. Most of the domestic migration to Florida has been from the Northeast and especially the New York area, which continues today. So unless Republicans are expecting to start breaking through among these types of white voters, there's probably a floor for Democrats here. At the very least, it's not a state where the GOP can continuously make huge gains among white voters without making huge gains among white voters nationally.

And if the GOP doesn't keep making huge gains among white voters—bigger gains than they're making nationally—Florida's going to go the same way as Nevada. The pace of demographic change in Florida should alarm Republicans. Think about it like this: Kerry lost Florida by 5 points in 2004. Then, Obama did 10 points worse among whites. All of this was countered and overwhelmed by demographic change and an improved showing among non-whites. Kerry's performance among white voters would have yielded a 7-point win in 2012—12 points better than his 5 point defeat in 2004.

If the trends of the last eight years continue, the white share of eligible voters will drop again, down to something like 63 percent of eligible voters. Some 300,000 new Hispanics will get registered to vote, and they'll break overwhelmingly for Democrats. If turnout patterns stayed the same, Republicans would need to win whites by 28 points to overcome demographic changes.

Could Republicans do four points among Florida whites in 2016, let alone keep increasing at that rate in future elections? Perhaps. But what a gamble! Surely even a GOP optimist would concede the serious possibility that they cannot improve by so much. Not after doing so well among Southern whites, not after running up the score against a candidate who was such a poor fit for the state. Not in a state where white voters are reminiscent of whites nationally.

Could a decline in black turnout help Florida Republicans? Perhaps, but not much. Black turnout only increased by

5 percent between 2004 and 2012, according to the census. More importantly, Florida is a state where the black share of eligible voters is increasing at a steady rate: According to the census, the state's black population increased by 22 percent over the last decade. The black share of eligible voters increased from 13 to 14.4 percent between 2004 and 2012. If that trend continues, it would cancel out almost all of the decline in black turnout. And if black turnout doesn't decline by as much as Republicans hope, the black share of the electorate could increase in 2016.

What about the missing white voters? They're not so helpful, either. According to the census, there were about 300,000 missing white voters in Florida. If they all turned out and voted for Republicans by 24 points, it would basically cancel out the demographic changes between 2012 and 2016, still leaving Republicans behind by about a point. Of course, whether the GOP can get all those voters back out is another question. And if the GOP narrowly wins by recapturing missing whites in 2016, they won't be able to count on another wave of missing whites to bail them out in 2020.

None of this means that the GOP couldn't win Florida in 2016. But there should be serious doubts about whether there's room for another round of big, additional gains among Florida whites. And once those doubts are raised, the GOP route to victory in Florida looks tough. They'd need a lot to break right in order to squeak out a victory in 2016, let alone afterward. There's the scary possibility that Florida goes the way of Nevada: the next Democrat would win Florida by 9 points if they merely did as well as Kerry among Florida's white voters.

Republicans probably can't return to Bush's performance among Hispanics, now that there are so many more Democratic-leaning Hispanics in Florida. But immigration reform would probably help. A Latino Decisions survey found that 39 percent of Florida Hispanics would be more likely to support a Republican who voted for immigration reform, higher than the 31 percent nationally. And although Florida Hispanics are less connected to the immigration debate than their Southwestern counterparts, more than 40 percent say they know an illegal immigrant. But even if the GOP would only make slight gains among Florida Hispanics, the pace of demographic change is so great that Republicans just can't afford to forfeit opportunities to improve in Florida. The stakes are too high. Florida is all but a must-win state for Republicans.

| "*Signing on to a comprehensive immigration package is probably part of one way for Republicans to form a winning coalition at the presidential level, but it isn't the only way.*"

Republicans Should Focus on Winning White Voters, Not Hispanic Voters

Sean Trende

Sean Trende is senior elections analyst for RealClearPolitics. He is a coauthor of The Almanac of American Politics 2014 *and author of* The Lost Majority: Why the Future of Government Is Up for Grabs—and Who Will Take It. *In the following viewpoint, he argues that Republicans do not need to appeal to Hispanic voters to stay electorally viable. He says that turnout of white voters dropped in the 2012 presidential election, probably because some working-class voters were turned off by Republican candidate Mitt Romney's pro-business stance. Trende suggests that if Republicans fielded a candidate who was more economically populist, that candidate could capture more white votes without doing significantly better among Hispanics.*

As you read, consider the following questions:

1. According to Trende, what was the drop in white votes from 2008 to 2012?

2. What specific policies of Ross Perot does Trende suggest would have appealed to working-class white voters?

3. Who does Trende say is the likely 2016 Democratic nominee, and how is that individual's appeal different from Barack Obama's?

With a cloture vote on the Senate's immigration reform bill expected next week [in June 2013], countless commentators have expressed the view that if Republicans don't sign on for reform, the party is doomed at the presidential level for a generation.

This is the first in a two-part series explaining why this conventional wisdom is incorrect. Signing on to a comprehensive immigration package is probably part of one way for Republicans to form a winning coalition at the presidential level, but it isn't the only way (for more, I've written a book about this, as well as countless articles here at RCP [RealClearPolitics]). Today I'll reexamine what was really the most salient demographic change in 2012: the drop-off in white voters. Next time, we'll confront some of the assumptions embedded in the "GOP [Grand Old Party, another name for the Republican Party] has to do this" argument head-on.

I should reemphasize at the outset that I think that embracing some sort of immigration reform probably helps with Republicans' outreach efforts to Hispanics, and the idea that there is a treasure trove of votes to be had for Democrats here is almost certainly overstated. I should also reemphasize that from a "pure policy" standpoint, I find quite a bit to like in the basic [immigration] "Gang of Eight" framework. But regardless of whether Republicans could or should back the bill, it simply isn't necessary for them to do so and remain a viable political force.

1. The most salient demographic change from 2008 to 2012 was the drop in white voters.

Let's start with the basics: Just what were the demographic changes in that four-year span? I did some preliminary work in November 2012 suggesting that the largest change came from white voters dropping out. Now, with more complete data, we can reassess this in a more precise manner.

Using the most commonly accepted exit-poll numbers about the 2008 electorate[1], we can roughly calculate the number of voters of each racial group who cast ballots that year. Using census estimates, we can also conclude that all of these categories *should* have increased naturally from 2008 to 2012, due to population growth.

From mid-2008 to mid-2012, the census estimates that the number of whites of voting age increased by 3 million. If we assume that these "new" voters would vote at a 55 percent rate, we calculate that the total number of white votes cast should have increased by about 1.6 million between 2008 and 2012.

The following table [shown in this viewpoint] summarizes these estimates for all racial groups, and compares the results to actual turnout.

Now, the raw exit-poll data haven't come out yet, so we can't calculate the 2012 data to tenths: The white vote for 2012 could have been anywhere between 71.5 percent of the vote or 72.4 percent (with 26,000 respondents, analysis to tenths is very meaningful). So the final answer is that there

---

1. Ruy Teixeira has mostly convinced me that the correct final exit numbers for 2008 were 74.3 percent white, 12.6 percent black, 8.5 percent Hispanic, 2 percent Asian and 2.6 percent "other."

Actual Versus Projected Turnout, 2008 to 2012, Based on Exits

	2008 Actual	2012 Projected	2012 Actual	Difference
White	97,677,100	99,139,605	93,033,145	(6,106,459)
Black	16,564,353	17,455,952	16,797,651	(658,301)
Hispanic	11,174,365	13,134,504	12,921,270	(213,234)
Asian	2,629,262	3,300,869	3,230,318	(70,551)
Other	3,418,041	3,910,201	2,584,254	(1,325,947)

TAKEN FROM: Sean Trende, "The Case of the Missing White Voters, Revisited," RealClearPolitics, June 21, 2013.

were 6.1 million fewer white voters in 2012 than we'd have expected, give or take a million.[2]

The Current Population Survey [CPS] data roughly confirm this. As I noted [in another article], if you correct the CPS data to account for over-response bias, it shows there were likely 5 million fewer whites in 2012 than in 2008. When you account for expected growth, we'd find 6.5 million fewer whites than a population projection would anticipate.

This is the real ballgame regarding demographic change in 2012. If these white voters had decided to vote, the racial breakdown of the electorate would have been 73.6 percent white, 12.5 percent black, 9.5 percent Hispanic and 2.4 percent Asian—almost identical to the 2008 numbers.

2. These voters were largely downscale, Northern, rural whites. In other words, Ross Perot voters.

Those totals are a bit more precise and certain (and lower) than my estimates from November of last year. With more

2. I also note that Hispanic participation probably exceeded projections when you consider that a disproportionate chunk of the Latino population growth consists of noncitizens who are therefore ineligible to vote. Also note the disproportionately large drop-off in "other"; I suspect this is mostly a function of the "rounding issue" I describe above.

complete data, we can now get a better handle regarding just who these missing white voters were.

Below [not included] is a map of change in turnout by county, from 2008 to 2012. Each shade of blue means that turnout was progressively lower in a county, although I stopped coding at -10 percent. Similarly, every shade of red means that turnout was progressively higher, to a maximum of +10 percent.

The drop in turnout occurs in a rough diagonal, stretching from northern Maine, across upstate New York (perhaps surprisingly, turnout in post–[Hurricane] Sandy New York City dropped off relatively little), and down into New Mexico. Michigan and the non-swing state, non-Mormon Mountain West also stand out. Note also that turnout is surprisingly stable in the Deep South; Romney's problem was not with the Republican base or evangelicals (who constituted a larger share of the electorate than they did in 2004).

For those with long memories, this stands out as the heart of the "Perot coalition" [when Ross Perot ran as an independent in 1992]. That coalition was strongest with secular, blue-collar, often rural voters who were turned off by [Democrat] Bill Clinton's perceived liberalism and [Republican] George H.W. Bush's elitism. They were largely concentrated in the North and Mountain West: Perot's worst 10 national showings occurred in Southern and border states. His best showings? Maine, Alaska, Utah, Idaho, Kansas, Nevada, Montana, Wyoming, Oregon and Minnesota. . . .

We're pretty confident that the voters were more likely to stay home if they resided in states that were hit by Hurricane Sandy, that were targeted by a campaign in 2008, that had higher foreign-born populations, and that had more Hispanic residents. The latter result probably suggests a drop-off in rural Hispanic voters, who are overrepresented in an analysis such as this one.

We're also pretty confident that the voters were more likely to turn out if they resided in counties with higher median household incomes, high population growth, a competitive Senate race in 2012, or that were a target state in 2012. Counties with higher populations of Mormons, African-Americans, and older voters also had higher turnout, all other things being equal. None of this is all that surprising.

Perhaps most intriguingly, even after all of these controls are in place, the county's vote for Ross Perot in 1992 comes back statistically significant, and suggests that a higher vote for Perot in a county did, in fact, correlate with a drop-off in voter turnout in 2012.

What does that tell us about these voters? As I noted, they tended to be downscale, blue-collar whites. They weren't evangelicals; Ross Perot was pro-choice, in favor of gay rights, and in favor of some gun control. You probably didn't know that, though, and neither did most voters, because that's not what his campaign was about.

His campaign was focused on his fiercely populist stance on economics. He was a deficit hawk, favoring tax hikes on the rich to help balance the budget. He was staunchly opposed to illegal immigration as well as to free trade (and especially the North American Free Trade Agreement). He advocated more spending on education, and even Medicare for all. Given the overall demographic and political orientation of these voters, one can see why they would stay home rather than vote for an urban liberal like President Obama or a severely pro-business venture capitalist like Mitt Romney.

3. These voters were not enough to cost Romney the election, standing alone.

But while this was the most salient demographic change, it was probably not, standing alone, enough to swing the election to Obama. After all, he won the election by almost exactly 5 million votes. If we assume there were 6.5 million "missing" white voters, that means that Romney would have had to win almost 90 percent of their votes to win the election.

Given that whites overall broke roughly 60–40 for Romney, this seems unlikely. In fact, if these voters had shown up and voted like whites overall voted, the president's margin would have shrunk, but he still would have won by a healthy 2.7 percent margin.

At the same time, if you buy the analysis above, it's likely that these voters weren't a representative subsample of white voters. There were probably very few outright liberal voters (though there were certainly some), and they were probably less favorably disposed toward Obama than whites as a whole. Given that people who disapprove of the president rarely vote for him (Obama's vote share exceeded his favorable ratings in only four states in 2012), my sense is that, if these voters were somehow forced to show up and vote, they'd have broken more along the lines of 70–30 for Romney.

This still only shrinks the president's margin to 1.8 percent, but now we're in the ballpark of being able to see a GOP path to victory (we're also more in line with what the national polls were showing). In fact, if the African-American share of the electorate drops back to its recent average of 11 percent of the electorate and the GOP wins 10 percent of the black vote rather than 6 percent (there are good arguments both for and against this occurring; I am agnostic on the question), the next Republican would win narrowly if he or she can motivate these "missing whites," even without moving the Hispanic (or Asian) vote.

4. The GOP faces a tough choice.

Of course, it isn't that easy. Obama won't be on the ticket in 2016, and the likely Democratic nominee, Hillary Clinton, could have a greater appeal to these voters (current polling suggests that she does). But there are always trade-offs, and

Clinton's greater appeal to blue-collar whites, to the extent it holds through 2016, could be offset by a less visceral attachment with young voters, college-educated whites and to non-whites than the president enjoys.

But the GOP still has something of a choice to make. One option is to go after these downscale whites. As I'll show in Part 2 [not included], it can probably build a fairly strong coalition this way. Doing so would likely mean nominating a candidate who is more Bush-like in personality, and to some degree on policy. This doesn't mean embracing "big government" economics or redistribution full bore; suspicion of government is a strain in American populism dating back at least to Andrew Jackson. It means abandoning some of its more pro-corporate stances. This GOP would have to be more "America first" on trade, immigration and foreign policy; less pro–Wall Street and big business in its rhetoric; more Main Street/populist on economics.

For now, the GOP seems to be taking a different route, trying to appeal to Hispanics through immigration reform and to upscale whites by relaxing its stance on some social issues. I think this is a tricky road to travel, and the GOP has rarely been successful at the national level with this approach. It certainly has to do more than Mitt Romney did, who at times seemed to think that he could win the election just by corralling the small business vote. That said, with the right candidate it could be doable. It's certainly the route that most pundits and journalists are encouraging the GOP to travel, although that might tell us more about the socioeconomic standing and background of pundits and journalists than anything else.

Of course, the most successful Republican politicians have been those who can thread a needle between these stances: Richard Nixon, Ronald Reagan and (to a lesser degree) Bush have all been able to talk about conservative economic stances without horrifying downscale voters. These politicians are rarities, however, and the GOP will most likely have to make a choice the next few cycles about which road it wants to travel.

"Those unmarried women present a huge opportunity for the Republican Party."

Republicans Should Improve Their Message to Women

Mary Kate Cary

Mary Kate Cary is a former White House speechwriter for President George H.W. Bush. She currently writes speeches for political and business leaders, and she is a contributing editor for U.S. News & World Report. *In the following viewpoint, she argues that Republicans do very poorly among women voters. However, she says, single women could be open to Republicans' message of economic responsibility, especially if Republicans are willing to slightly moderate their position on issues such as abortion. Cary concludes that Republicans quickly need to improve their outreach to American women.*

As you read, consider the following questions:

1. According to the viewpoint, what does Stan Greenberg say about the party identification of single women?

Mary Kate Cary, "Single and Ready to Mingle with the GOP," *U.S. News & World Report* online, January 31, 2013. www.usnews.com. Copyright © 2013 U.S. News & World Report LP. All rights reserved. Reproduced with permission

2. How does Cary suggest Republicans appeal to women who are risk averse?

3. What does Cary believe Republicans should say on abortion to appeal to young women?

It's been well documented that the gender gap in the 2012 presidential election was big—CNN reported women backed [Barack] Obama by 55 percent, [Mitt] Romney 44 percent—and this was the fifth straight presidential election that Democrats enjoyed a double-digit lead among women voters. When you add up the difference between the men's and women's votes, there was an 18-point gender gap and a 41-point "marriage gap" between the candidates as well. According to Karlyn Bowman of the American Enterprise Institute, unmarried voters tend to vote Democratic, married ones tend to vote Republican. Those unmarried women present a huge opportunity for the Republican Party.

Address Single Women

The proportion of unmarried women is growing. "Unmarried" can mean never married, widowed, or divorced, but the majority of unmarried women are single and young. Ruy Teixeira of the Center for American Progress estimates that unmarried women now represent 47 percent of all American women; in 1970, only 38 percent were unmarried. Demographer Wendell Cox found that, in 2008, states with the highest percentage of childless women under 45 tended to vote Democratic.

But Democratic pollster Stan Greenberg told the Daily Beast, just before the election, that unmarried women are not particularly partisan: "They're for Obama, it's not a whim, but it's not party identification. . . . If you're looking for people who call themselves Democrats, it's not them." Greenberg went on to say that unmarried women felt their issues were ignored by Obama, especially in the debates, and that hurt him. There's a lesson there: If Republicans want to win more elections at both the state and national level, then they need to start addressing the concerns of young, single women.

Take the economy. Mitt Romney picked up support for women after his first debate when he framed economic growth as a women's issue. Polls consistently show that women rank concern for the economy and jobs above other issues by wide margins. Women especially are concerned about leaving a fiscal mess for the next generation. Put in that context, Republicans have a good message when it comes to reining in government spending, bringing Medicare and Medicaid back to sustainability, and reducing the federal deficit.

But instead of only addressing working families, Republicans should target their economic message to single women—specifically, young working women who are trying to make ends meet. Many of them are concerned about getting their first job in a tough economy. Once they're hired, they're understandably worried about their job security. They're burdened by the double whammy of student debt and higher taxes; they're troubled by rising prices taking a bite out of the money they're trying to save. There's an opening for a fiscally responsible, pro-growth, opportunity-oriented message aimed at young, working female voters. Many of these women will end up starting their own businesses and, at least in theory, should be Republican voters.

Government, Guns, and Abortion

Bowman also notes that while polls show—and the Julia video from the Obama campaign reinforced—that women are more likely to favor an activist government with a guarantee of health care and social services, women are more risk-averse than men. Many young women may think putting their retirement savings, for example, in a private investment account tied to the stock market is "risky" compared to Social Security—but Republicans should make clear that entrusting one's

Women and the 1996 Election

For years, critics of the women's movement had argued that a broad-based women's vote was a myth. They claimed that women were no more homogeneous than men and that gender was overemphasized in determining how a woman voted. While it is obvious that women are diverse, this argument failed to recognize that women's awareness of the condition and needs of their gender could be a unifying political force.

In 1996 the argument was unmasked. A majority of women of different backgrounds came together in a voting consensus that proved there was a women's voting bloc of sufficient consequence to determine the outcome of a presidential election. And the catalyst that brought them together was not their trust of [Democrat] Bill Clinton but their distrust of the Republican Party.

Tanya Melich,
The Republican War Against Women:
An Insider's Report from Behind the Lines.
New York: Bantam, 1998.

retirement to a wasteful, inefficient government that is going bankrupt is actually one of the most dangerous financial decisions a woman can make.

There's an opportunity for Republicans, too, when it comes to young women and protecting the rights of gun owners. While Democrats like to point out the large gender gap that exists on the question of gun control—women are more supportive of gun control than men—they forget that not everyone who owns a gun looks like [former Republican vice president] Dick Cheney. According to CBS News, the total number of female gun owners nationally has doubled over the last decade. (In fact, there's a "huge demand" for pink guns, according to *Guns & Ammo*, magazine.) A 2010 story in the *Washington Times* cited a study that found 80 percent of female gun owners had purchased the guns for self-defense. While many women want universal background checks and mandatory gun safety training, not everyone agrees that all guns are evil. It's more complicated than the Left thinks, and there's an opening for Republicans to take the side of women who want to defend themselves.

Surprisingly, there is very little gender difference when it comes to attitudes about abortion: majorities of both men and women think it should be legal under certain circumstances. But I do think if Republicans would soften their rhetoric on abortion, they'd do well with younger unmarried women as well. The party should remain opposed to abortion, but leave room for compassion when women are the victims of rape, incest, and life-threatening situations. Being "pro-life with exceptions" would allow young women who are morally uncomfortable with abortion but who don't want to overturn *Roe v. Wade* to feel they have a political home. Right now, they don't.

Young women are not a monolithic voting bloc. The party that treats them as vital contributors to a strong economy, as citizens who can create a better life for everyone, as empowered souls who can overcome adversity, and as bright minds who will be our future leaders will win their votes. Republicans should move quickly.

| *"Being a conservative is all about facing hard truths, and the fundamental hard truth about dating is that the best strategy is the simplest one: Just Be Yourself."*

The Match.com Theory of GOP Marketing

Fred Schwarz

Fred Schwarz is a writer for National Review. *In the following viewpoint, he argues that the Republican Party is not organized to appeal to disparate groups. Rather, he says, conservatism is about telling hard truths and staying true to one's self. Republican policy positions are right, and intelligent people, he suggests, will see that. Therefore, tailoring a distinctive message for women will not work for the Republican Party and will cause the Grand Old Party (GOP) to betray itself. Instead, Republicans should trust in women's intelligence and present them with the same policy arguments it presents to everyone else.*

As you read, consider the following questions:

1. According to the viewpoint, what advice does the Growth and Opportunity Project offer to Republicans about attracting women's votes?

2. What does Schwarz mean when he says that the Democratic Party is a political party in the classic sense?

3. What points does Schwarz say Republicans should sell to women just as to everyone else?

We've been hearing a lot lately about how Republicans need to improve their appeal to women, especially unmarried ones. Commentators offer various advice; a longtime Republican strategist says "GOP congressional leaders should unveil a comprehensive women's agenda" and "legislation that has a positive [message] that will help female voters in an attempt to soften their image." The RNC's [Republican National Committee's] much-hyped Growth and Opportunity Project cautions that:

> Republicans need to talk about people and families, not just numbers and statistics. . . . Women need to hear what our motive is. . . . Those are things that cannot be communicated well in graphs and charts—and we need to do a better job communicating why our policies are better, while using female spokespeople to do it.

And pollsters agree that single women are the key segment.

Although I'm no political consultant, I may be able to help with this, because before my recent marriage, I spent several decades trying to appeal to single women, with a distinct lack of success. I wouldn't exactly say I learned a lot about them; if I had, it wouldn't have taken so long to get married (or at least it wouldn't have seemed so long). But I did learn a lot about what doesn't work, and one thing I figured out pretty quick is that unmarried women know when someone is trying to feed them a line. They may know and not care, but they know.

And a lot of the ideas being offered for how the GOP can appeal to women make the party sound like an eager but clumsy bachelor: "Oh, you're female? Well, you must be interested in stuffed animals—and wait till I tell you about Senator Graham's Stuffed Animal Subsidy Initiative. . . ." That level of sincerity gets you the nice-try smile and the suddenly remembered morning appointment.

On the other hand, I've heard reports of guys getting good results by appealing to a woman's intelligence. For some reason, this never worked very well for me (perhaps it was the bowtie), but I'm told it can be quite successful if you at least sound sincere.

What all this suggests is that the Republican Party's appeal to women should be the same as its appeal to everyone. Are girls not supposed to be interested in a bunch of boring budget numbers because math class is tough? If she doesn't know the difference between a million, a billion, and a trillion, she's probably a committed Democrat anyway.

Among other things, the GOP is not built for making narrowly focused appeals. So when people say the party should adopt such-and-such policy initiative, or soften its opposition to so-and-so, in order to capture women's votes, it's like a consultant telling a silverware company that their spoons will appeal to a whole new market if they turn them into sporks.

The Democrats are a political party in the classic sense, a coalition of disparate interests that unite to scratch each other's backs and pick everyone else's pockets. But granting special favors to specific groups is contrary to conservatives' core beliefs, so even if some clever operative came up with a killer Free Market Grrrlz platform, the rank and file's hearts would not be in it—and when your heart is not in the right place, just as when your eyes are not in the right place, women can tell. Trust me on that.

Being a conservative is all about facing hard truths, and the fundamental hard truth about dating is that the best strategy is the simplest one: Just Be Yourself. This applies even when yourself is a guy who recites the 1988 Pittsburgh Pirates' batting order at parties and decorates his apartment with

Doctor Who bobblehead dolls—because when you try to be somebody else, not only will you do a lousy job of it, but even if somehow your imitation is true to life, the character you're playing probably isn't what she's looking for either.

So the best way for the GOP to appeal to women is to Just Be Yourself. Sell fiscal responsibility, individual freedom and initiative, law and order, market-based solutions, a strong defense, and all the other points that distinguish our beliefs from the Democrats' "but wait, there's more!" sales pitch. Respect women's intelligence, trust them to be smart enough to appreciate sound policy, and don't expect to win them over with shiny gifts that you had to hock your principles to afford.

Oh, and do ditch the bowtie.

| "The kindly, nice, personally average evangelical voter is the most dangerous person in America."

Evangelicals Are to Blame for Republican Culture-War Extremism

Frank Schaeffer

Frank Schaeffer is the author of Crazy for God: How I Grew Up as One of the Elect, Helped Found the Religious Right, and Lived to Take All (or Almost All) of It Back. *In the following viewpoint, he argues that evangelicals' faith has led them to doubt science and fact. As a result, he argues, they have been easy dupes for nonsensical Republican ideology, including the denial of global warming and the support for Israel abroad despite its unjust policies. He concludes that evangelical gullibility will eventually doom the Republican Party and perhaps the country.*

As you read, consider the following questions:

1. According to Schaeffer, who funds the Republican Party?

2. According to the viewpoint, what does Andrew Cuomo say is a factual statement?

   3. Why does Schaeffer believe the evangelical/Republican
      Party/billionaire alliance is doomed?

Not all evangelicals are right-leaning Republicans. But according to polls, 73 percent are. That's the folks I'm talking about here.

No one sane disputes the fact that the *base of the base* of the Republican Party—post [the Supreme Court decision protecting abortion] *Roe v. Wade* and with a big "assist" from my late religious-right-leader father Francis Schaeffer and me (before I changed my mind)—is evangelical voters. No one sane disputes the fact that the Republican Party is funded these days mainly by a handful of billionaires with a vested interest in seeing that government does their economic will. No one sane disputes the fact that this attempt to work the billionaires' economic will has little to nothing to do with the core "family values" and "pro-life" issues that motivate the vast swath of right-wing-leaning evangelical voters. And no one sane disputes the fact that in the old days voters disagreed over policy but mostly agreed on basic facts from which policy would be derived.

Not any more.

Evangelicals and Science

These days the Right disputes the facts from how life evolved to unemployment numbers to where the president was born. For instance, the right disputes the reality of climate change and our human contributions to that change. Evangelicals have mostly signed up for this often-oil-and-coal-companies-funded alternative view of "reality" because their theology teaches them to reject the "world" and look for some other explanation of the cosmos and everything in it than that offered by science.

In other words, for those who reject the science of evolution—or reject the science on how people become heterosexual or homosexual, or the economic facts as to why women have abortions (48 percent fall below the poverty line), or what an embryo is, or if the biblical account is literally true and so on—it is easy to embrace other alternative "explanations." This is especially true for those who see themselves as an embattled persecuted minority of victims of "liberalism."

The alternative "explanations" about how the world works are offered to evangelicals eager to have their faith confirmed by their own "experts." Enter those with their own agendas eager to dupe the dupeable. Enter the neoconservatives, the crazies saying that President [Barack] Obama isn't a real American. Enter the [libertarian philosopher] Ayn Rand–worshipping gun-fondling libertarian Tea Party or those saying that gays "choose" their "lifestyle," an explanation offered by hacks, quacks and bigots. These "facts" all have something in common: They are sold to the gullible by self-interested liars. And nothing conditions you to be gullible more than biblical literalism.

These liars specializing in lying to the gullible these days include oil-and-coal-company-paid "scientists" denying climate change and paid hack "therapists" offering to change gay men and women into heterosexuals.

The liars are mostly Republican operatives (of the Ralph-Reed-bottom-dwelling ilk) shilling for the likes of the Koch brothers [referring to wealthy, pro-Republican brothers Charles and David Koch], the oil and coal companies and the Far Right of the Republican Party with its neoconservative warmongers. These self-interested parties have discovered that the biblical, literalist evangelicals are very, very easy prey. You see speaking as one raised in the evangelical subculture I know that people like me were raised believing in imaginary truths. So we are perfect folks to sell yet more "alternative" realities to.

These new "truths" range from climate change denial to the idea that Israel is a great little country that can do no wrong and that no matter how many wars we get into in the Middle East defending a bunch of crazed Zionists illegally occupying the West Bank that it's okay because those wars are somehow a "fulfillment of prophecy."

Hurricane Sandy

But the problem Republicans and evangelicals share is that while American elections can be bought by secret money, reality itself intrudes from time to time. Enter New York City and New Jersey underwater [after Hurricane Sandy in 2012].

As Timothy Egan writes in the *New York Times*

> "Climate change is to the Republican base what leprosy once was to healthy humans—untouchable and unmentionable. Their party is financed by people whose fortunes are dependent upon denying that humans have caused the earth's weather patterns to change for the worse.
>
> "At the same time, Republicans have spent the last year trying to win an argument about the role of government as a helping hand. By now, most people know that [2012 Republican presidential candidate] Mitt Romney, in his base-pandering mode during the primaries, made the federal disaster agency FEMA [Federal Emergency Management Agency] sound like a costly nuisance, better off orphaned to the states or the private sector.
>
> "His party can get away with fact-denial—in global warming's case—and win cable-television arguments about FEMA, so long as something like a major news event, e.g., reality, does not shatter the picture. That's where the storm upset a somewhat predictable race."

"There has been a series of extreme weather incidents," said New York Gov. Andrew Cuomo, stating the obvious. "This is not a political statement. This is a factual statement. Anyone who says there is not a dramatic change in weather patterns I think is denying reality."

The other cherished idea of Republican/evangelical matrix (with a few handy Mormons and conservative Roman Catholics thrown in) scattered by Sandy's winds is the idea that people don't need government. Let the local church volunteers handle it!, the cry goes up.

But when the bill for New Jersey's recovery comes due, no state or church group will pay. And when each year our "once in a generation" disasters hit again and again and again, don't turn to your local climate-change denier for help.

As Egan put it:

> "Ayn Rand is having her *Mad Men* [a television show set in the 1960s] revivalist moment in the Republican Party, led by social Darwinists like Paul Ryan. These people genuinely do believe that life is a battle between achievers and moochers, and that luck, good or bad, has little to do with it. Compassion is for wussies, and tax dollars from those at the top should not be used to help those who are struggling.
>
> "Of late, we've seen the 'hate of all nature,' as one old-timer called the Dust Bowl, visit nearly every part of the United States. Texas was on fire for much of a year while its governor, Rick Perry, denied climate change and signed an official proclamation calling for a day of prayer for rain."

Evangelical Beliefs

Here's what the evangelicals on the right have embraced:

- An alternative version of reality from creationism to denial of global warming

- The "fact" that Jesus will soon return so that none of this matters anyway

- The "fact" that America must always defend Israel because the "Bible says so"—even as Israel slides into becoming an apartheid state that will be submerged by its own structural Zionist injustice to Arabs and may take its "greatest ally" (the USA) down with it

- The refusal to embrace gay rights

- The whites-in-charge mentality, even as demographics change and America becomes a brown country

- The circle-the-wagons, head-in-the-sand home "school" movement pitting individuals against their communities

- The odd alliance with the NRA [National Rifle Association] and "gun rights" by Christians who say they follow the Jesus who said "turn the other cheek"

- The retributive version of war as a way of life to punish the world for "not liking" us

- The acceptance of the lies and outright racism of the shrill anti-Obama [conservative network] Fox News–type reaction to a black man in the White House . . .

Touch it where you may, the evangelical/Republican Party/billionaire alliance is doomed; it's doomed because the non-retributive Jesus is the true Lord, not a hate-filled ideology of imperial overreach that is embraced by crazed and militarized right-wing neoconservatives.

It's doomed by immigration-pattern demographics; it's doomed by nature as we lose our coastal cities one at a time and people remember who it was—folks like the Koch brothers and their evangelical foot soldiers—who made this possible by denying global warming; it's doomed by the fact that other countries not waiting for the return of Jesus, building high-speed rails and embracing science and simple facts will leave us in the dust; and it's doomed because lies of the magnitude accepted by the evangelicals and the right about reality will eventually run into the truth. Or the truth will run into them, and—literally in the case of global warming—wash them away.

Dangerous Dupes

To the extent that the alternative evangelical-theological reality has turned evangelical voters into suckers for the "gospel" of the oil companies and coal companies and neoconservatives, the kindly, nice, personally average evangelical voter is the most dangerous person in America.

These nice folks next door—soup kitchens and good works notwithstanding—will destroy the reality we all are stuck with while trying to force-feed "facts" to the country that are lies on behalf of people who will be living in gated communities in the Rockies while average Americans watch our prairies burn and our cities wash away. And when we finally bankrupt ourselves fighting Middle East wars on behalf of crazed Zionists occupying the West Bank, drill our last oil well in a national park, and discover that we're in a self-created Apocalypse, it will be too late to note that Jesus didn't return to yank idiots to heaven out of the mess they made, and the only sound you'll hear is the great grandchildren of some very stupid and deluded people cursing their memory.

Meanwhile President Obama is going to win reelection [in 2012]. The Republican Party will dwindle and the evangelicals' role in politics will become a hissing and a byword. And I'm betting that the evangelicals will learn nothing from this, just circle the wagons for their last stand against not just their fellow Americans but against reality herself. Good luck with that.

And to the extent that an "act of God"—tropical storm Sandy—may have helped President Obama win reelection, how very hilarious. I mean weren't Mormons and evangelicals united in praying against our first black president?

I feel sorry for God. With his "friends" helping the Republicans to screw up our planet for profit, he's in as much trouble as the Republican Party is. God needs better friends, and evangelicals need a better theology.

I say again: Touch it where you may, the evangelical/Republican Party/billionaire alliance is doomed; it's doomed because the non-retributive Jesus is the true Lord, not a hate-filled ideology of imperial overreach that is embraced by crazed and militarized right-wing neoconservatives and the haters of not just our first black president but of God and his good earth.

> *"Recent polls have found younger evan-gelicals drifting away from some of the conservative views of their parents and grandparents."*

Evangelical Leader Preaches Pullback from Politics, Culture Wars

Neil King Jr.

Neil King Jr. is the Wall Street Journal's *global economics editor. In the following viewpoint, he reports on Russell Moore, the principal public voice for the Southern Baptist Convention, the leading American evangelical group. Moore, unlike his predecessors, has tried to de-emphasize culture-war issues such as same-sex marriage and has tried to emphasize that Christians are not devoted to partisan political struggles. King says that most evangelicals remain Republicans and that Moore himself is very conservative. Nonetheless, King concludes, evangelicals seem to be moving to moderate their very close relationship with the Republican Party and their intense focus on political issues.*

As you read, consider the following questions:

1. Why does Mark DeMoss say Republicans are finding it hard to get evangelicals together for political purposes?

2. According to King, with what political issues is Moore actively involved?

3. What does King suggest is significant about Moore's meeting with Reverend Joe Phelps?

For years, as the principal public voice for the Southern Baptist Convention, the country's biggest evangelical group, Richard Land warned of a "radical homosexual agenda" and pushed for a federal ban on same-sex marriage.

His successor, Russell Moore, sounded a different note when the Supreme Court in June struck down the federal Defense of Marriage Act. "Love your gay and lesbian neighbors," Mr. Moore wrote in a flier, "How Should Your Church Respond," sent to the convention's estimated 45,000 churches. "They aren't part of an evil conspiracy." Marriage, he added, was a bond between a man and a woman, but shouldn't be seen as a "'culture war' political issue."

Since the birth of the Christian-conservative political movement in the late 1970s, no evangelical group has delivered more punch in America's culture wars than the Southern Baptist Convention and its nearly 16 million members. The country's largest Protestant denomination pushed to end abortion, open up prayer in public schools and boycott Walt Disney Co. over films deemed antifamily. Its ranks included many of the biggest names on the Christian right, including Pat Robertson and Jerry Falwell.

Today, after more than three decades of activism, many in the religious right are stepping back from the front lines. Mr. Moore, a 42-year-old political independent and theologian who heads the convention's Ethics and Religious Liberty Commission, says it is time to tone down the rhetoric and pull back from the political fray, given what he calls a "visceral recoil" among younger evangelicals to the culture wars.

"We are involved in the political process, but we must always be wary of being co-opted by it," Mr. Moore said in an interview in his Washington office, a short walk from Congress. "Christianity thrives when it is clearest about what distinguishes it from the outside culture."

Along with much of the religious right, Southern Baptists are undergoing a generational shift as Mr. Moore and his allies recalibrate their methods and aims. The moment is significant not only for America's religious life but for its politics, given the three-decade engagement by evangelical leaders that kept social issues on the front burner and helped Republicans win national elections.

Self-described evangelicals still vote heavily Republican. Exit polls show that nearly eight in 10 sided with Mitt Romney in the 2012 presidential election, a larger share of that group than either of the previous two Republican nominees received.

But Republican operatives with ties to the evangelical movement say much is changing. Every year tens of thousands of evangelicals, particularly the young, leave the Southern Baptist and other big denominational churches for more loosely organized assemblies that oppose abortion but are less likely to hew to other Republican causes.

"Republicans are finding it increasingly hard to collar evangelicals for political purposes, simply because the movement is so fragmented now, so decentralized, and a growing number of evangelicals simply find politics distasteful," says Mark DeMoss, a former chief of staff to Mr. Falwell and an adviser last year to Mr. Romney's campaign.

Mr. Moore is responding to this drift. He warns evangelicals to avoid becoming "mascots for any political faction." He focuses on how to keep millennials engaged in the church. His advice to church leaders: Be "winsome, kind and empathetic."

His advice meshes with those in the Republican Party who want the GOP to back off hot-button cultural issues to stress themes such as job creation and education. Party leaders earlier this year released a manifesto calling for the GOP to become more tolerant, welcoming and inclusive. The shift also comes as Republicans face a growing rift in the party between its activist tea-party flank and its more traditional business wing.

Mr. Moore and other prominent Christian conservatives are blunt in conceding that their long quest to roll back the sexual revolution has failed. The fight, they say, sowed divisions within the movement and alienated young believers.

"I would characterize the movement as having experienced a very tough defeat that now requires a shift of tactics," says Ralph Reed, who ran the once-powerful Christian Coalition through the 1990s. Religious conservatives once promised imminent victories, he says, "but we are now looking at 50- and 75-year horizons."

Some evangelical leaders compare the moment today to the retreat that followed the 1925 Scopes "Monkey trial" over Tennessee's effort to limit the teaching of evolution in public schools. The trial led to a public backlash against evangelicals.

"Evangelicals felt a sting from the culture after the Scopes trial that they weren't used to feeling," says Mark Dever, an ally of Mr. Moore and pastor of the Capitol Hill Baptist Church. "What is happening now with evangelicals is a disabusing of any idea of a simple victory of the right in a fallen world. They realize that is not going to happen."

The change in approach, which not all evangelical groups or churches share, isn't without risk. Albert Mohler, a top voice in the church as president of the Southern Baptist Theological Seminary in Louisville, Ky., and a Moore mentor, says the transition to a less confrontational approach, which he supports, could alienate church members from its leaders.

"When Richard Land spoke to most issues, he was certain that Southern Baptists were behind him and he was their mouthpiece," Mr. Mohler says. "Russ will need a deft touch to make sure that Southern Baptists stay behind him."

Mr. Moore is in no way a liberal. He equates abortion with the evils of slavery, considers homosexuality a sin, and insists the Southern Baptist Convention will never support gay marriage. At the same time, he emphasizes reconciliation and draws a traditional doctrinal distinction between the sinner and the sin.

Southern Baptists still make up more than a third of all the country's Protestant evangelicals, by far the largest single denomination under that umbrella, which itself comprises more than a quarter of the U.S. population. But their primacy is on the wane.

Baptists are departing from the religious traditions of their childhood faster than any other Protestant group, according to statistics gathered by Pew Research, an independent polling organization. Adult baptisms within Southern Baptist churches, meanwhile, have slid 20% over the past decade, according to LifeWay Research, a polling firm tied to the Southern Baptist Convention. The firm projects the church's membership will fall by half to 8.5 million by 2050, returning to the level of the mid-1950s.

Recent polls have found younger evangelicals drifting away from some of the conservative views of their parents and grandparents. A March survey of nearly 1,000 white evangelicals by the Public Religion Research Institute, a nonpartisan polling organization, found half of those under 35 favored same-sex marriage, compared with just 15% of those over 65. The younger evangelicals were more likely to be independents over Republicans, while the opposite was true of their elders.

"The religious right was born on the theology of numerical expansion: the belief that conservative churches grow while

Democrats and Evangelicals

The question is why many evangelicals have moved rather decisively toward Republican loyalties over the past few decades. My answer is pretty basic. Republicans have opened key political positions to evangelicals (although nowhere close to the proportion of their vote), maintain a positive view of people of faith in general and evangelicals in particular, and reflect the beliefs of most evangelicals on abortion and other "values" questions. Democrats could do all these things and recapture a significant percentage of the evangelical vote, but they choose to appeal to other constituencies instead. Nothing wrong with that; every political party has to make these decisions. However, when Democrats adopt positions they know will alienate many evangelicals, no one should be shocked when evangelicals align with the other party.

Steve Wilkens and Don Thorsen,
Everything You Know About Evangelicals Is Wrong (Well, Almost Everything): An Insider's Look at Myths and Realities. *Grand Rapids, MI: Baker Books, 2010, p. 158.*

liberal ones die. That conceit is gone now," says David Key, director of Baptist Studies at Emory University's Candler School of Theology.

Mr. Moore would like the Southern Baptists to be able to hold on to people such as Sarah Parr. The 31-year-old social worker grew up in a conservative Southern Baptist family in southern Virginia. She graduated from Liberty University, founded in 1971 by the Falwell family. But she says she found herself increasingly less at home in the church, and left it altogether in her 20s.

She now attends a nondenominational church that meets in an old theater on Washington's Capitol Hill. Politically, she describes herself "as a moderate at best, if I'm anything. But I don't find myself in either party."

When Mr. Moore took over in June as the Southern Baptists' top public-policy advocate, he startled some in the church by declaring as dead and gone the entire concept of the Bible Belt as a potent mix of Jesus and American boosterism. "Good riddance," he told thousands of the faithful at the group's annual convention in Houston in June. "Let's not seek to resuscitate it."

In an essay for the conservative Christian magazine *First Things*, titled "Evangelicals Retreat?," he dinged the movement for "triumphalism and hucksterism" and lampooned a time when its leaders dispatched voter guides for the Christian position on "a line-item veto, the Balanced Budget Amendment, and the proper funding levels for the Department of Education."

Mr. Moore says there is no doctrinal daylight between him and his church, and he insists he isn't seeking to return the Southern Baptists to a past in which it shunned politics entirely.

He travels almost weekly from his home in Nashville to Washington to meet with members of the Obama administration and with congressional leaders. He has allied with the Roman Catholic Church and other religious groups to make the case that overhauling the U.S. immigration system is a Christian goal. He is pushing the Pentagon to give religious chaplains in the military freer rein to preach, and has helped build a new coalition to fight a federal requirement that insurers provide contraception coverage.

His approach, however, is strikingly different from that of his predecessor Mr. Land, who for a quarter century served as the leading voice of the Southern Baptists. Like many evangelical leaders of his generation, Mr. Land, a Princeton-educated Texan, openly aligned himself with the Republican Party and popped up frequently in the Oval Office during the George W. Bush years.

Long before their divergent approaches on the gay-marriage issue, Messrs. Moore and Land split over the huge rally held by conservative talk-radio host Glenn Beck in front of the Lincoln Memorial in August 2010. Mr. Land attended the rally as Mr. Beck's guest, and later compared Mr. Beck to Billy Graham, calling him "a person in spiritual motion."

Mr. Moore, in an essay posted after the rally, said the event illustrated how far astray many conservative Christians had wandered in pursuit of "populist God-and-country sloganeering and outrage-generating talking heads."

In an interview, Mr. Land said the Southern Baptist leadership is divided into those who think the culture war is lost; those who are weary and want it over; and those who think they are losing the war but feel victory is still possible. He declined to say where he puts Mr. Moore, but said he counts himself among the latter. "We are like where Britain was in 1940, under heavy attack but still not defeated," he said.

Asked to respond, Mr. Beck in a written statement applauded Mr. Land and said, "In times like these, we need to find common ground."

Mr. Moore grew up with a Catholic mother and a Baptist father in a working-class, heavily Democratic neighborhood in Biloxi, Miss. His paternal grandfather was a Baptist pastor. He went every summer on Baptist Bible outings, and gave his first youth sermon when he was 12. ("It was dreadful," he recalls. "I vomited before and after.")

Through college he worked for Rep. Gene Taylor, a Democratic freshman congressman from Mississippi who later gave him a Bible signed by President Bill Clinton, which he now keeps in his home. He calls his vote for Mr. Clinton in 1992 "a great mistake," and says he "loved" George W. Bush. He remains a registered independent.

Mr. Moore has pushed to patch up rifts within the Baptist movement between the conservative Southern Baptist Convention and a growing number of more liberal breakaway groups. While still living in Louisville, he met repeatedly for coffee with Rev. Joe Phelps, the liberal pastor of the city's Highland Baptist Church, which welcomes openly gay and lesbian members. The church broke from the convention in 2002.

"He respects me and acknowledges that I am living out my Christian convictions," Rev. Phelps says, "while others in the movement might not even recognize that I am a Christian."

Speaking at his inauguration in mid-September, Mr. Moore told the gathering of congressmen, pastors and church leaders to look beyond trying to save American culture. One day, he said, "the monuments to American power" that dot the Washington landscape will be in ruins. While continuing to fight for justice, he said to a rumble of agreement, "we must also remember that we are not Americans first. We belong to another kingdom."

Periodical and Internet Sources Bibliography

The following articles have been selected to supplement the diverse views presented in this chapter.

John Blake	"Like GOP, Evangelicals Look to Rebrand," CNN—*Belief Blog*, March 26, 2013.
David Callahan	"As Evangelicalism Declines, Is the GOP Toast?," Demos, December 26, 2013.
Michelle Cottle	"The Elephant Trainer: Christine Toretti Is on a Quest to Make the GOP the Party of Women," *Atlantic*, March 2014.
David M. Drucker	"Recognizing Danger, GOP Engages with Democrats in Battle for Women Voters," *Washington Examiner*, April 23, 2014.
Ilyse Hogue	"How the GOP Can Win Back Women," MSNBC, April 27, 2014.
Josie Huang	"Republicans on Mission to Win Over Asian-American Voters," Southern California Public Radio, February 10, 2014.
Ina Jaffe	"Will Seniors Leave Republicans Out to Dry in 2014?," NPR, December 9, 2013.
Jennifer Sevilla Korn	"The GOP Explains Its Plan to Build 'A Home for Latino Voters,'" *Huffington Post*, April 18, 2014.
Alex Roarty	"RNC Chairman Downplays Gender Gap," *National Journal*, March 18, 2014.
Sabrina Schaeffer	"Engage, Disrupt, Win: How Republicans Can 'Finally' Win Women Voters," *Forbes*, April 29, 2014.

OPPOSING
VIEWPOINTS®
SERIES

CHAPTER 3

What Issues Divide Republicans?

Chapter Preface

In 2010 a right-wing conservative movement known as the Tea Party began to play an important part in Republican electoral politics. Since then, there has been tension between Tea Party Republicans and mainstream Republicans, prompting some commentators to argue that the Republican Party may be falling apart.

For example, Abby D. Phillip in a December 12, 2013, report on ABC News quoted a conservative as saying that the party was in a "full-scale civil war." Phillip went on to describe House Speaker John Boehner's frustration with Tea Party legislators who, he said, had pushed the party to shut down the government in a futile effort to defund the Patient Protection and Affordable Care Act and health care reform. Boehner accused the Tea Party members of "misleading their followers" and said "they've lost all credibility." Tea Party activists lashed back; Daniel Horowitz, policy director of the conservative Madison Project, said ominously, "There can be no reconciliation between those who seek power for power's sake and those who seek to serve in order to restore our Republic."

Elias Isquith in an October 11, 2013, article at Salon.com, argues that these internal divisions will eventually split the Republican Party in two. Isquith says that the Tea Party politicians are driven by a vision of America in decline and have no interest in compromise. On the other hand, the mainstream Republican Party is mostly devoted to business interests, wants to pass legislation, and is not interested in absolutist stances. For instance, the 2013 government shutdown, which the Tea Party embraced, cost many businesses money. "The GOP [Grand Old Party], quite simply, has been split in two," Isquith concludes, and he suggests that the Tea Party may become a separate third party.

Other writers, however, are less convinced that Republican internal arguments spell doom for the GOP. Andy Kroll in an April 7, 2014, article in *Mother Jones* notes that its divisions do not seem to be hurting the Republican Party as it prepares for elections in 2014 and 2016. Political scientist Jonathan Bernstein goes further in an April 7, 2014, post at Bloomberg and argues that there really is not a Republican civil war at all. "That doesn't mean that there aren't policy disagreements within the Republican Party," Bernstein says. "But these disagreements are far less intense than, say, the battles between liberal and conservative wings of the party in the 1950s and 1960s." Bernstein believes that the Tea Party's refusal to compromise makes it difficult for the Republican Party to govern, but it seems unlikely to have much effect on its ability to win elections or on the stability of the Republican Party as a whole.

The viewpoints in the following chapter examine disputes within the Republican Party over issues such as immigration, health care reform, and climate change legislation.

> "What's needed in the House now is not a favor for Obama, but a strong conservative answer on one of the most vexing issues facing the nation."

Immigration Reform Would Help GOP

Tamar Jacoby

Tamar Jacoby is president and chief executive officer of Immigra-tionWorks USA, a national federation of small business owners in favor of immigration reform. In the following viewpoint, she says that there is some support among House Republicans for immigration reform. She says Republicans need to recognize that failing to move on immigration will hurt the party and the country. She further maintains that Republicans should move forward and lead on the issue rather than let immigration reform be associated with President Barack Obama and the Democrats.

As you read, consider the following questions:

1. According to Jacoby, more and more House Republicans understand what two things about immigration reform?

2. What does Jacoby believe is the fallout of the budget battle for immigration reform?

3. Who is Aaron Schock, and what is his view of immigration reform, according to Jacoby?

The government's open. Washington is back at work. House Republicans, licking their wounds, are asking themselves what's next. And President Barack Obama has thrown down the gauntlet: The top item on his agenda is immigration reform.

What are the chances that the House will now move ahead on immigration? The answer will have less to do with immigration than with how the budget battle has changed the larger political dynamic in Washington.

House Republicans' views on immigration are untested, and many advocates for reform believe they are implacably hostile. But the truth is Republican opinion has been evolving since the 2012 election. More and more House Republicans, perhaps the majority, know that reform is overdue and that the GOP [Grand Old Party, another name for the Republican Party] must be part of the solution—to remain competitive with Latino voters and because it's the right thing to do.

Individual lawmakers and essential staff continued to work on the issue even through the dark days of the shutdown. And members are coalescing around answers to the hardest of the hard questions: What to do about immigrants living in the United States illegally? House majority leader Eric Cantor is working on a bill that would create a path to citizenship for "Dreamers" [referring to individuals who meet the general requirements of the Development, Relief, and Education for Alien Minors (DREAM) Act] brought to the U.S. illegally as children.

And one recent informal count found 84 House Republicans—more than one-third of the total—in favor of legal status for the Dreamers' parents.

Bottom line: If it weren't for the rancor of the budget brawl, the House might be in a good place on immigration, with Republicans ready to move forward and pass a package of measures they could send to a conference with the Senate bill.

Opinion: Key to immigration reform—Worker visas

So what exactly is the fallout from the budget battle?

Surprisingly, it appears to cut both ways—both for and against the prospect of an immigration overhaul.

Even before the government reopened, two different factions were making their voices heard. Some, such as Rep. Raúl Labrador of Idaho—an opponent of the budget deal but a strong proponent of immigration reform—argued that the budget battle had made it hard, if not impossible, for House Republicans to reach a deal with Obama.

Others, such as Rep. Aaron Schock of Illinois, who voted for the budget package, said it's time to get back to the give and take of governing—time to sit down with Democrats and compromise, including on immigration.

Opinion: It's not Syria holding up immigration reform

Which of these two sentiments will prove stronger in the House? GOP lawmakers are reeling from their recent drubbing. Skepticism and negativity are at an all-time high. And it will take both kinds of champions—tough-minded and accommodating—to negotiate a deal. But if enough other Republicans agree with Schock and make their views known, that could empower leadership to open the way to consideration of some immigration bills.

A handful of hard-line conservatives—the group that opposed the budget deal—still hold enormous sway in the House. And just because Speaker John Boehner waived the so-called Hastert Rule once—bringing the legislation that ended the shutdown up for a vote when he knew it lacked support from the majority of the Republican majority—doesn't mean he'll do that again anytime soon. The House Republican con-

Republican Anti-Migrants

Among Republicans we have a new generation of politicians such as Senators Ted Cruz and Marco Rubio who are quickly emerging as a new class of conservative Latino politicians across the United States. These two particular cases are emerging as the Latino face of the anti-migrant bloc in what is a transparent attempt to recast the image of Republicans as being inclusive and to lend credence to the claim that anti-migrant policies are color-blind. In fact, just seven months after the 2012 election, Republicans in the House of Representatives have sponsored a bill to defund the DACA program [Deferred Action for Childhood Arrivals program, which gives relief to immigrants who come to the US as children] and to increase funding for the DHS's [Department of Homeland Security's] detention and deportation programs. The main spokesman in the Senate against the immigration reform in the 113th Congress was Senator Ted Cruz, who proposed poison amendments to remove any pathway toward citizenship in the 2013 Senate immigration bill. Cruz, a Tea Party Republican who is to the "right" of even Senator Rubio, has appeared on *The Rush Limbaugh Show* and other conservative talk radio programs to boost opposition to the immigration bill. Rubio has also called for expanding the "border fence" and threatened to revoke his support from the very bill that he helped draft if certain border triggers are not met. Politicians like Cruz and Rubio are not going away; in fact, conservative Latinos like them are being groomed across the country. They will become the new face of the anti-migrant bloc for years to come.

Alfonso Gonzales, Reform Without Justice:
Latino Migrant Politics and the Homeland Security State.
New York: Oxford University Press, 2014, p. 157.

ference is only as strong as it is cohesive, and the majority-of-the-majority rule has proved a good way to maintain that power and cohesion.

Still, the complex dynamic that drives Republicans in the House may have shifted somewhat in the shutdown. Certainly you hear a lot more grumbling, in private and in public, about the power of the hard-line naysayers. Other members are tired of being held hostage. Many want to get on with governing, making deals on a wide range of issues. And a few, such as Schock, are starting to say so, even on TV.

Opinion: How Obama can clinch immigration deal

That's a ray of hope. But there's still another danger looming.

The one thing House Republicans are not going to do in the wake of the budget battle—not on any issue, in any circumstances—is a favor for Obama. And to the degree that immigration reform is seen as Obama's issue, it will be dead on arrival in the House.

The question for House Republicans, leadership and rank and file: Do they want to cede the issue to Obama? Can they afford to let him own it? More and more of the GOP grasps that that's a mistake. It's a disaster politically for the party and a mistake for the nation, which needs reform, urgently, for the sake of the economy and the rule of law.

What's needed in the House now is not a favor for Obama, but a strong conservative answer on one of the most vexing issues facing the nation.

Will House Republicans see it that way? Can they take ownership and move forward?

> *"If Mitt Romney had won a record-shattering 70 percent of the Hispanic vote in 2012, he still would have lost the election."*

Immigration Reform Will Not Help Republicans with Hispanic Voters

Arnold Ahlert

Arnold Ahlert was an op-ed columnist with the New York Post *for eight years and currently writes for JewishWorldReview.com and FrontPageMag.com. In the following viewpoint, he argues that even if Republicans pass immigration reform, Hispanic voters will still distrust the party. Furthermore, he says Hispanics do not even support immigration reform. Finally, he argues that there are fewer Hispanic individuals in the electorate than Democrats claim. For all these reasons, he says, Republicans should not change their position on immigration reform and should focus on border security rather than on a path to citizenship.*

As you read, consider the following questions:

1. What is the bright news for Republicans in the poll Ahlert discusses?

2. In the last fifty years, what Republican candidate received the highest total of the Hispanic vote, and what was it, according to Ahlert?

3. Why doesn't Ahlert believe that Hispanics are natural Republican voters?

If the rumors coming out of Washington, DC, are accurate, amnesty will die a long, slow death in the House of Representatives. According to *Politico*, Republican leaders got together yesterday to plan how they would deliver the news to the public. The current thinking among the House resisters was best expressed by Rep. Steve King (R-IA), who represents those most adamantly opposed to the legislation. He insisted the Senate plan is about helping "elites who want cheap labor, Democratic power brokers, and those who hire illegal labor." "It would hurt Republicans, and I don't think you can make an argument otherwise," he added.

No Benefit to GOP

On Monday [July 8, 2013], House Speaker John Boehner (R-OH) reiterated a point he has made many times before, namely that he has no plans to take up the Senate bill in his chamber. "The House is going to do its own job on developing an immigration bill," he said. "The American people expect that we'll have strong border security in place before we begin the process of legalizing and fixing our legal immigration system."

It is not just the American people in general who want strong border security to be put in place before anything else is passed. A new survey taken by GOP [Grand Old Party, another name for the Republican Party] pollster John McLaughlin reveals that a large majority of *Hispanic* voters believe the border should be 90 percent secure before any legal status is granted to illegal aliens. Registered Hispanic voters backed that proposal by a margin of 60 percent to 34 percent, while Hispanic adults in general backed the proposal by a 60 percent to 32 percent margin. Hispanic voters also opposed granting illegal aliens the ability to obtain federal benefits, including health care, while they are going through the process of legalization, and before the 90 percent goal is achieved, by a margin of 56 percent to 40 percent.

There was a divergence between registered and non-registered voters regarding two other issues. Employment verification to determine the status of potential employees was supported by 64 percent of registered voters, compared with just 46 percent of non-registered Hispanics. Increased border security was approved by 55 percent of registered voters, but only 45 percent of non-registered voters.

Yet the most telling part of the poll was a repudiation of the idea "comprehensive immigration reform" would constitute some sort of political redemption for Republicans. A whopping 65 percent believe that the Republican Party discriminates against Latinos and Hispanics, 61 percent believe the Republican Party doesn't care about people like them, and 62 percent believe Republicans are against immigration because they don't want any more Hispanics in the country.

If there is a bright side, only 29 percent said they would never vote for a Republican, and 46 percent agree with the statement that there are "new forces in the Republican Party like Senator Marco Rubio who are fighting for immigration reform and fair treatment for Latinos." Yet 39 percent still believe "it is the same old Republican Party and is as prejudiced as always against Latinos."

Thus, despite all the media, squishy Republican, and Democratic hoopla attempting to convince Republicans that they are "doomed" if they fail to pass this package, their battle to win the hearts and minds of Hispanics is *still* an uphill battle at best. Furthermore, it may not be a battle worth winning if it alienates their base. As the *Huffington Post's* Charles Babington explains, "Republicans will go nowhere if they lose a hard-core conservative every time they pick up a new un-aligned voter with a more moderate message."

Hispanics Overcounted

Yet more importantly, Republicans have lost sight of the big picture in two ways. First, as journalist Steven Sailer reveals, Census Bureau data, taken after every national election, show exit polls following the 2012 election overstated the share of the Hispanic vote—just as they have done in every election since 2000. And not just the exit polls. Sailer notes the main-stream media also exaggerated the Hispanic share of the 2012 vote by a factor of almost 20 percent. In fact, the percentage of Latinos casting ballots declined from 49.9 percent in 2008 to 48 percent in 2012, and the number of Hispanics who claimed to be eligible but didn't bother to vote jumped from 9.8 million to 12.1 million. Thus, the overall Hispanic vote in 2012 accounted for only 8.4 percent of the total, not the 10 percent as originally reported.

Furthermore, no Republican presidential candidate has won a majority of the Hispanic vote in more than 50 years. George W. Bush reached the highest percentage in that span of time, getting 40 percent in the 2004 election. Even after Ronald Reagan signed the Simpson-Mazzoli bill [officially known as the Immigration Reform and Control Act] in 1986, granting unambiguous amnesty to 2.7 million illegal aliens, the Republican share of the Hispanic vote actually declined from 37 percent to 30 percent in the 1988 election. Yet despite that reality, George H.W. Bush won in a landslide.

In other words, the pernicious notion that the Hispanic vote is critical to Republican success has been grossly exagger-ated, a reality made evident by Byron York. York revealed that if Mitt Romney had won a record-shattering *70 percent* of the Hispanic vote in 2012, he still would have lost the election.

The other part of the big picture Republicans have lost sight of revolves around the idea disseminated by the estab-

Party Seen as Closer to Own Views on Immigration

Just your opinion, which political party's policies on immigration and immigration reform come closer to your own—the Democratic Party or the Republican Party?

	Democratic Party %	Republican Party %	Neither (vol.)/ No Opinion %
US Adults	48	36	17
Non-Hispanic Whites	41	42	16
Blacks	70	14	16
Hispanics	60	26	13

(vol.) = Volunteered response
June 13–July 5, 2013.

TAKEN FROM: Lydia Saad, "In U.S., More Relate to Democrats than GOP on Immigration," Gallup, July 15, 2013.

lishment wing of their own party, which has promoted the idea that Republicans should vote for comprehensive reform because Hispanics are essentially "natural Republicans" who just don't realize it yet. This is unadulterated nonsense. Hispanics overwhelmingly support Obamacare [the Patient Protection and Affordable Care Act] by a margin of 62 percent, and big government by a margin of 75 percent, rising to 81 percent among Latino immigrants. Politically speaking, 30 percent of them are self-described liberals, compared to 21 percent of the general population. And, according to the Pew Research Center, 55 percent of Hispanics have a negative view of capitalism, higher than white and black Americans.

None of those are remotely "natural Republican" positions.

Health Care and the Economy

That doesn't mean Republicans should write off the Hispanic vote. The same McLaughlin survey mentioned above notes that immigration reform isn't as important to Hispanics as health care, which ranked second, and the economy, which is issue number one. The rapidly unraveling health care bill is so corrosive to Democrats that the president has kicked the rule of law to the curb and unilaterally postponed the employer mandate by one year to get through the 2014 election. Republicans should make a pitched effort to offer *every* ethnic group a viable alternative. As for the economy, the current official unemployment rate for Hispanics is 9.1 percent, compared to 7.6 percent for the nation as a whole. Thus, Republicans must also make the case that legalizing at least an additional 11 million illegal aliens—a number many consider a low estimate—will make it even harder for Hispanic citizens to find jobs.

More importantly, Republicans need to realize that the public in general has no use for a Senate immigration bill that has been revealed as a complete fraud with regard to border control. Virtually every aspect of it can be waived by the secretary of homeland security, absent any repercussions. This reality flies in the face of a CNN/ORC international survey that finds 62 percent of Americans believe border security should be the main focus of U.S. immigration policy, compared to just 36 percent who want a so-called pathway to citizenship for illegal aliens to be the foremost priority.

Yet the most likely reason the Senate bill will die in the House can be boiled down to one word: comprehensive. Comprehensive reform, whether it is 2,400 unread pages of comprehensive health care reform or 1,190 unread pages of comprehensive immigration reform, is riddled with special political deals, exceptions, loopholes, and waivers—all of which can be manipulated with impunity.

Much to their overwhelming dismay, a majority of Americans have discovered the disturbing details of Obamacare, *after* it was passed, exactly as Democrats intended. House Republicans have no incentive whatsoever to repeat that folly, given the realities of the Hispanic vote's current impact, the fact that many of their members represent districts with insignificant levels of Hispanic population, and the possibility that the results of the midterm election in 2014 may put them in a far better bargaining position than they are in now.

Furthermore, the fact that border control as a stand-alone policy is completely anathema to Democrats should tell them everything they need to know about the pitfalls of comprehensive immigration reform. If enacted now, it will be carried out by a president with no respect for the separation of powers, an attorney general presiding over the most racially polarized Justice Department in memory, and a clueless DHS [Department of Homeland Security] secretary.

On Wednesday, White House press secretary Jay Carney said that passing a comprehensive immigration reform bill has "always been an uphill battle." If House Republicans care about the future of the nation, it should stay that way until a *genuinely* sensible series of reforms—each standing *individually* on its own merits—can be enacted.

> *"Our critique must be about the law in its entirety—the negative impact it will have on our health care system and the way in which it substantially increases costs to pay for the benefits it claims to provide."*

Obamacare Will Fail Without Any Help from Republicans

Lanhee Chen

Lanhee Chen is a Bloomberg View columnist. A research fellow at the Hoover Institution who also teaches public policy at Stanford University, he was the policy director of Mitt Romney's 2012 presidential campaign. In the following viewpoint, he argues that Republicans should stop trying to repeal President Barack Obama's health care reform using government shutdowns and should instead allow it to be implemented so that the bad effects of the law become clear to the American public. At that point, he says, Republicans will be in a position to gain sweeping electoral advantages. He contends that insurance premiums under Obamacare, or the Patient Protection and Affordable Care Act, will rise rapidly, alienating many voters.

As you read, consider the following questions:

1. According to Chen, what was the token concession Republicans won after the government shutdown?

2. According to the viewpoint, what specific predictions about premiums does Avik Roy make?

3. What parts of Obamacare are popular, according to Chen?

Now that we've ended the two-week-old government shutdown [in 2013] and avoided the calamity of a default on our sovereign debt obligations, political pundits are debating who won and who lost. The better question is, what should Republicans do next?

It's charitable to say that Republicans "didn't win" this battle, as House Speaker John Boehner conceded. Those who insisted Obamacare [referring to the Patient Protection and Affordable Care Act] must be defunded ended up with only a token concession from Democrats: a requirement that the secretary of health and human services "certify" that those receiving the Patient Protection and Affordable Care Act's government subsidies to purchase health insurance are actually eligible for them.

But did Republican tactics permanently compromise their ability to capitalize on the deeply flawed rollout of Obamacare and what many analysts (myself included) believe will be its deleterious impacts on the U.S. health care system? Not necessarily. Republicans can still use Obamacare's failings to their advantage, but it will require a disciplined, realistic approach. And it means recognizing the impossibility of large-scale changes to the law while Barack Obama is president.

Failed Tactics

First, this week's agreement to reopen the federal government and raise the debt limit means we will find ourselves back in

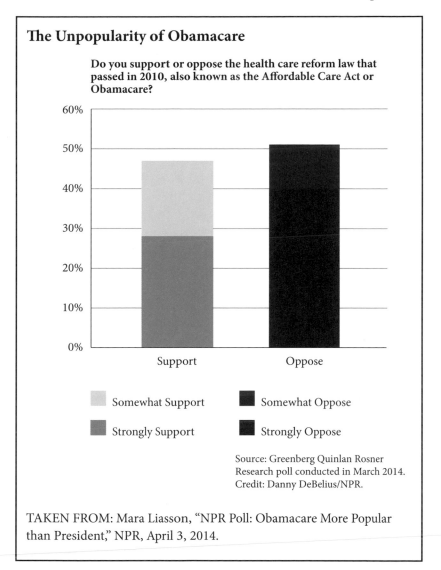

The Unpopularity of Obamacare

Do you support or oppose the health care reform law that passed in 2010, also known as the Affordable Care Act or Obamacare?

Support | Oppose

Somewhat Support · Somewhat Oppose
Strongly Support · Strongly Oppose

Source: Greenberg Quinlan Rosner Research poll conducted in March 2014. Credit: Danny DeBelius/NPR.

TAKEN FROM: Mara Liasson, "NPR Poll: Obamacare More Popular than President," NPR, April 3, 2014.

this situation again early next year. The temptation among some conservatives—particularly those who fought to defund Obamacare—will be to again make extravagant demands of Democrats in exchange for either keeping the government open or raising the debt ceiling again.

The tactic didn't work this time, and it won't work next time, either. President Obama and Senate Democrats have made it clear that they are not only unwilling to compromise on broader Republican demands to delay or defund the law, but also are unwilling to budge on more limited changes, such as delaying implementation of the individual mandate or putting off some of the tax increases that help to fund Obamacare. Republicans would be wise to completely decouple the debt-ceiling and government-funding issues from their efforts to alter or eliminate Obamacare.

Second, the best way for people to see how bad the health care law will be is, in many respects, to get out of the way. Two of the Obama administration's most prominent (and politically popular) promises about the law—that it would reduce health insurance premiums and that people who like their coverage can keep it—will continue to go unfulfilled.

Avik Roy and his colleagues at the Manhattan Institute [for Policy Research] have estimated, for example, that 27-year-old men who were able to purchase basic health insurance plans before Obamacare will pay, on average, almost 100 percent more for similar plans next year. Similarly, 27-year-old women will see their premiums increase an average of 55 percent. The news isn't much better for 40-year-old men and women, who will also see substantial increases in their premiums next year because of the law. Other studies have similarly concluded that Obamacare will drive up premiums not only for individuals purchasing insurance, but also for many small employers who provide coverage to their employees.

A number of additional Obamacare provisions threaten to displace millions of Americans from the health care coverage and doctors they know and like. This is because Obamacare gives employers financial incentives to scale back or terminate coverage, and it places additional coverage mandates on individual health insurance plans that will result in narrower networks of providers and hospitals, or the elimination of existing plans.

Finally, Republicans must remain focused on the damage that will be done by the entirety of the law rather than trying to engage President Obama and his allies on individual components of the law. There are components of Obamacare that are very politically popular, such as the blanket restriction on insurers denying coverage to those with preexisting medical conditions and allowing children up to age 26 to remain on their parents' health insurance plans.

Opportunity Squandered

Republicans must not get bogged down in debates about the merits of individual elements of the law. Instead, our critique must be about the law in its entirety—the negative impact it will have on our health care system and the way in which it substantially increases costs to pay for the benefits it claims to provide.

Our party squandered a golden opportunity this month to focus the American people on Obamacare's shortcomings and the ways in which its implementation and rollout has been an utter disaster. Over the next several months, they will have new opportunities to describe, demonstrate and highlight just how bad the law is. If they play their cards right, and bring public pressure to bear on the president and other supporters of Obamacare, they might actually force Democrats to consider the wisdom of standing behind a law that's clearly failing.

> *"The 2017 Project with which we're associated has developed an alternative to Obama's 2,700 pages of federal largesse."*

Republicans Need to Offer an Alternative to Obamacare

William Kristol and Jeffrey H. Anderson

William Kristol is the founder and editor of the Weekly Standard. *Jeffrey H. Anderson is a former senior speechwriter for Secretary Mike Leavitt at the US Department of Health and Human Services and a senior fellow in health care studies at the Pacific Research Institute. In the following viewpoint, they argue that there is a strong conservative alternative to Obamacare, officially known as the Patient Protection and Affordable Care Act. They point to the plan of the 2017 Project, with which they are associated. The plan promises to insure more people, deal with preexisting conditions, and lower health insurance costs. It will also, they say, make certain that no one is forced to buy health insurance and that people who like their health insurance can keep it. They conclude that their plan provides a blueprint for repealing and replacing Obamacare.*

As you read, consider the following questions:

1. How do the authors say their plan will increase the number of people with insurance without forcing anyone to buy anything?

2. Though most Americans don't support income redistribution, what do they support, according to the authors?

3. What winning claim do the authors say their proposal allows conservatives to make?

Obamacare [referring to the Patient Protection and Affordable Care Act] is failing. Faced with this unpleasant reality, President [Barack] Obama offered up during his State of the Union address his only remaining defense of his eponymous program: There is no alternative. "[M]y Republican friends . . . if you have specific plans . . . tell America what you'd do differently. . . . We all owe it to the American people to say what we're for, not just what we're against."

An Alternative

We accept the challenge. The 2017 Project, with which we're associated, has developed an alternative to Obama's 2,700 pages of federal largesse. The proposal builds upon prior efforts by conservative policy makers and thinkers, including recent proposals from the House Republican Study Committee (RSC) and a trio of senior GOP [Grand Old Party, another name for the Republican Party] senators (Tom Coburn, Richard Burr, and Orrin Hatch). It would solve the three core problems that called out for real reform even before the Democrats passed Obamacare: getting more people insured; dealing with the problem of preexisting conditions; and lowering costs. In providing politically attractive and substantively sound solutions to these three core concerns, it would justify bringing an end to Obamacare, and thus would pave the way for full repeal.

Just as important as what our proposal would do is what it wouldn't do. It wouldn't force anyone to buy insurance. It wouldn't auto-enroll anyone in any plan. It wouldn't reduce the tax break for employer-based insurance (aside from closing the tax loophole at the high end). It wouldn't cost anywhere near the $2 trillion over a decade that Obamacare would cost. It wouldn't undermine religious liberty. It would allow Americans to keep their current plan if they like it.

In order to increase the number of people with insurance versus the pre-Obamacare status quo without compelling anyone to buy anything, the 2017 Project proposal would address what has long been a basic unfairness in the tax code. Why should millions of Americans who get insurance through their employer get a tax break, while millions who buy it on their own through the individual market do not? We would end this unfairness by offering a refundable tax credit, one that would apply to everyone who buys insurance through the individual market (just as the employer-based tax break applies to everyone in the employer market). Since insurance costs increase with age, the value of the tax credit does too: $1,200 for those under 35 years of age, $2,100 for those between 35 and 50, and $3,000 for those who are 50 or over. There would also be a $900 credit per child. Those who didn't use the full value of their tax credit could deposit what's left in a health savings account (HSA). Figures from the Government Accountability Office suggest that—in the absence of Obamacare's myriad mandates—such credits, combined with the reform of letting people buy insurance across state lines, would make a low-premium ("catastrophic") policy affordable for everyone.

Obamacare's taxpayer-funded subsidies are substantial for the near poor and some of the near elderly, but they do virtually nothing for most of the young or the middle class. Obamacare's neglect of these two rather significant groups opens up a huge political vulnerability. A 2017 Project study of Obamacare's subsidies in the 50 largest American counties shows that a typical 26-year-old man who makes $35,000 would get no Obamacare subsidy whatsoever for the cheapest-priced "bronze" plan. Nor would a 36-year-old woman who is making that same $35,000. Under our alternative, by contrast, they would get tax credits of $1,200 and $2,100 respectively, which they wouldn't have to use for a government-run "exchange" plan but could use for any plan they'd like.

Helping the Poor and Middle Class

While most Americans don't support Obamacare's income redistribution, they also don't want to see those with lower incomes tossed off their newly acquired insurance. In terms of effects on the near poor and the middle class, the two most recent GOP alternatives tend to err in opposite directions. The RSC proposal relies on a tax deduction, not a credit. So it provides a significant assist to the upper half of income earners, while millions of lower-income people would get comparatively little help in paying for their insurance. The Coburn-Burr-Hatch proposal, on the other hand, income-tests its tax credit, therefore doing little or nothing for much of the middle class. Our alternative effectively splits this difference, offering tax credits rather than deductions, but not means-testing them—thus helping both the newly insured near poor and the neglected-by-Obamacare middle class.

To solve the problem of expensive preexisting conditions, our alternative would allocate $7.5 billion a year in defined-contribution federal funding for state-run "high risk" pools. Through such pools, anyone could buy affordable, partially subsidized insurance, and no one could be turned away because of a preexisting condition. We also propose (1) that no one could be dropped from, or re-priced by, their existing insurance—including insurance purchased under Obamacare—because of a preexisting condition; (2) that those who turn 18 (or leave their parents' insurance) have a one-time, one-year buy-in period during which they couldn't be denied coverage, or charged more, for a preexisting condition—and that parents be granted a similar one-year buy-in period for newborns; and (3) that people be able to move from employer-based plans to individual plans, or between individual plans of the same level, without being denied coverage, or being re-priced, for a preexisting condition.

There's more to our proposal, and we invite readers to take a look at it at www.2017project.org. We're certain it's not perfect, and we hope others will find ways to improve upon it. But we do think it sketches a compelling alternative to Obama-care, one that should allow Americans to have confidence in what would follow repeal. For this proposal can make the following winning claim: under this conservative alternative, health costs would drop, liberty would be secured, and any American who wants to buy health insurance would be able to do so. And we can be freed from the nightmare of Obama-care.

"Conservatives have the answer to energy and climate—it's free enterprise and fixing market distortion."

Republican Thinkers Launch New Climate Change Initiative

Coral Davenport

Coral Davenport covers energy and environment policy for the New York Times *and formerly for the* National Journal. *In the following viewpoint, she reports on efforts by Republicans to develop a market-based strategy to address climate change. Davenport says that the Republican position at the moment is mostly to deny that climate change is occurring and block any effort to pass legislation addressing the regulation of carbon emissions. However, some Republican lawmakers, policy makers, and special interest groups are trying to develop market-based solutions for climate change, such as a tax on fossil fuels, to be offset by cuts in income taxes and other taxes that conservatives dislike.*

As you read, consider the following questions:

1. What caused former congressman Bob Inglis to be on the outs with the right wing of the Republican Party, according to Davenport?

2. Why does Davenport say that insurance companies might support climate change legislation?

3. What reason does Grover Norquist give for opposing a tax on fossil fuels?

A small cadre of big-name Republican thinkers, disturbed by their party's stance on climate change, are engaging in a nationwide campaign, launching on Tuesday [in July 2012], to persuade the GOP to embrace "conservative solutions" to global warming.

Energy and Enterprise Initiative

Over the past two years, Tea Party groups and fossil-fuel-funded super PACs [political action committees] have driven the GOP [Grand Old Party, another name for the Republican Party] far to the right on global warming, as more Republicans question climate science or recant their former support of climate policy. That's led to a rift between moderates and hard-line conservatives—emblematic of a larger divide in the party—as some moderate Republicans fear that rejecting climate change could lead their party to be branded as anti-science.

The Energy and Enterprise Initiative, based at George Mason University, aims to unite moderate Republicans concerned about climate change with hard-line fiscal conservatives who want to cut taxes and government spending. It's led by former Rep. Bob Inglis, R-S.C., who has been on the outs with the right wing of his party since he lost his 2010 primary as a direct result of his support for climate change policy.

On its own, Inglis's voice might not be enough to change the Republican conversation about climate change. But he has the support of Gregory Mankiw, economic advisor to the [2012 Republican] Mitt Romney campaign and the former chief economist of President George W. Bush's Council of Economic Advisers; Douglas Holtz-Eakin, president of the influential conservative think tank American Action Forum, former head of [George H.W.] Bush's Council on Economic Advisers, and economic adviser to John McCain's 2008 presidential campaign; Art Laffer, the prominent conservative economist and former senior adviser to President [Ronald] Reagan; and George Shultz, Reagan's secretary of state, along with a slew of other conservative economic thinkers.

Mankiw, Romney's advisor, has long been a leading advocate of this policy—although the Romney campaign declined to answer whether Romney himself would support it. Though Mankiw isn't expected to give speeches on behalf of the new campaign, given his involvement with Romney, Inglis described Mankiw as an "ally." And in an e-mail to *National Journal*, Mankiw wrote, "I am supportive of this effort."

Laffer, however, has already given one speech, at Vanderbilt University, supporting the policy. Last year, Holtz-Eakin held living-room meetings about climate change with New Hampshire voters.

Taxing Fuel

The campaign will push one policy: a new tax on carbon pollution or gasoline consumption, paired with a cut in the income or payroll tax, creating a revenue-neutral, market-driven solution to an environmental problem while cutting taxes that conservatives dislike.

The idea is essentially to create a tax that will discourage fossil fuel use and pollution while eliminating a tax in order to incentivize work and income. It's an old idea that environmentalist and former vice president Al Gore also has supported, but one that conservative economists say could be reborn in next year's effort to pass a sweeping tax-reform package.

The campaign will send conservative thinkers across the country to speak about the policy to conservative audiences,

The GOP and Climate Change

Turning from popular opinion to the opinions of politicians, views on climate change have been unstable recently. The science of climate change has not undergone a revolution in the last few years, but there has nevertheless been a great increase in the voice of climate change deniers among national political figures. At the time of the 2008 presidential election, both major political parties in the United States had come to the conclusion that climate change was happening. Of the two parties, there is no doubt that the Democratic Party has historically been less skeptical about climate change than has the Republican Party. Indeed, it is easy to get the impression that the Republican Party does not believe climate change is happening at all. This impression, however, is wrong—or at least, it was wrong in 2008. Just the opposite was true at the time. If one judges from their official party platforms, the Republicans and the Democrats had both come to the conclusion that human activity was causing our planet to warm.

During the 2008 presidential campaign, Senator John McCain, the Republican candidate, was on the record as believing that climate change was indeed man-made. Within his party, McCain was hardly alone. The official party platform stated:

The same human economic activity that has brought freedom and opportunity to billions has also increased the amount of carbon in the atmosphere.

Andrew T. Guzman,
Overheated: The Human Cost of Climate Change.
New York: Oxford University Press, 2013, p. 27.

such as gatherings of college Republicans, members of the Federalist Society, or the annual Conservative Political Action Conference.

"Conservatives have the answer to energy and climate—it's free enterprise and fixing market distortions," Inglis told *National Journal.* "Entrepreneurs and investors will deliver the fuels of the future. It will be faster and more efficient than government. It's just a matter of conservatives stepping forward and engaging rather than retreating into denial about science, which is a strange place for us to be."

The initiative will be a tough sell in today's hotly partisan political climate, where any proposal of a new tax—let alone an energy tax—is explosive. But the moderates see an opening for the argument in a coming effort to overhaul the nation's tax code, a debate in which conservatives will push to cut income, payroll, and corporate taxes.

And in addition to the big-name GOP economists, the proposal may also find backing in other, surprising quarters: ExxonMobil, the nation's biggest oil company, has backed a carbon tax. The campaign also will work with insurance companies—long-standing allies of the Republican Party, but also a group which must take into account the projected impacts of climate change, such as property damage caused by rising sea levels and increased flooding.

Michael McKenna, a Republican energy lobbyist and strategist who works closely with House GOP leadership on energy policy, predicted that the push is likely to gain traction on the Hill.

"I think it has the potential to be important, mostly because people who would oppose them are kind of asleep at the switch," McKenna wrote in an e-mail. "It is also clearly an attempt to prepare for whatever sort of conversation we are going to have about tax reform in the next however many years."

Still, McKenna said Republicans are likely to encounter plenty of problems in the details of the proposal.

"It suffers from a real lack of specifics," he wrote. "If you work the math, it looks like this: We use about 140 billion gallons of gasoline each year, and the payroll tax brings in about 750 billion each year. I realize that there are other things that would get taxed in such a regime, but if you simplify it, it looks like it would take a $5 a gallon tax on gasoline to clear the same amount of money. The guys who favor this never talk specifics, and now I know why—the specifics are incredibly unappetizing."

National Journal attempted last year to survey congressional Republicans on their views on climate change. Sixty-five GOP lawmakers—40 House members and 25 senators across the ideological spectrum—agreed to respond.

Twenty of the 65 Republicans said they think climate change is causing the earth to warm; 13 said that climate change isn't causing the earth to warm; and 21 said they didn't know, the science isn't conclusive, or they didn't want to answer the question definitively. Nineteen said that human activities do contribute to climate change—but of those 19, only five said they believed a "significant amount" of climate change was due to human activity, while 14 said they believed human activity contributes "very little" to climate change. Five said they believed that climate change was not at all attributable to human activity.

Norquist Opposition

The biggest obstacle will likely be opposition from influential conservative lobbyist Grover Norquist, president of the group Americans for Tax Reform, who has signed 539 Republican lawmakers and candidates onto a pledge promising never to raise taxes.

"Even a revenue neutral swap would be an extremely bad move for taxpayers," Norquist told *National Journal*. "It would create a new tax that would certainly grow over time—name a tax that didn't . . . and the old tax that was pruned back, would also grow again."

He called the initiative "a very bad idea for taxpayers and is clearly being pushed by advocates of ever-larger government . . . with a possible assist from 'conservatives' who have no sense of history."

The true measure of the campaign's success will be whether the issue is championed by key Republican lawmakers, who will have to agree to push for it as part of a tax reform package as well as stand by it on the campaign trail.

One key Republican with sterling conservative fiscal chops is already doing just that—with backing from an influential Tea Party group. Rep. Jeff Flake, R-Ariz., the current favorite to become Arizona's next senator next year, supports the idea. In 2009, he coauthored a bill with Inglis to create a carbon tax paired with a cut in the payroll tax. And the bill won backing from the head of the Arizona chapter of Americans for Prosperity, the influential Tea Party group with ties to the oil company Koch Industries.

Another possible backer is Sen. Lisa Murkowski of Alaska, the senior Republican on the Senate Energy and Natural Resources Committee.

Environmentalists and the White House are watching the effort closely. After President Obama's effort to move a cap-and-trade climate change bill through Congress died—and contributed to the losses of many incumbent Democrats in Congress in 2010—Democrat-led efforts to push climate policy are likely to face a wall of opposition in the coming years. Strategists say an effort led by Republicans—a "Nixon goes to China"-type moment [referring to Richard Nixon's trip to Communist China in 1972]—is likely the only chance for moving climate policy before 2016.

"This is an important step. If the U.S. is ever going to get a carbon tax, it has to have a conservative address," said Joshua

Freed, director of the clean energy program at Third Way, a Democratic think tank. "For this to morph from an aspiration into a policy contender, we need the heft of Republicans who hold office and are weighing the impact of reelection to settle in."

| *"If Congress is serious about job creation and economic growth, it should drive back the regulation of GHGs [greenhouse gases]."*

Conservatives in Congress Should Not Pass Climate Change Regulation

Nicolas Loris

Nicolas Loris, an economist, focuses on energy as well as environmental and regulatory issues as the Herbert and Joyce Morgan fellow at the Heritage Foundation. In the following viewpoint, he argues that the link between fossil fuel emissions and climate change is uncertain. He says that Environmental Protection Agency (EPA) efforts to regulate carbon emissions or greenhouse gases (GHGs) are based in poor science and on dubious legality. He also says that in the United States, and worldwide, regulation of carbon emissions will harm economic growth and restrict development. He concludes that Congress should pass laws preventing the EPA from implementing any regulations on carbon emissions.

Nicolas Loris, "Congress Should Stop Regulations of Greenhouse Gases," The Heritage Foundation online, September 23, 2013. www.heritage.org. Copyright © 2013 The Heritage Foundation. All rights reserved. Reproduced with permission.

As you read, consider the following questions:

1. According to Loris, what have climate models failed to predict in regard to global temperatures?

2. Why does Loris believe it is immoral to urge developing countries to reduce carbon emissions?

3. What three actions does Loris recommend to Congress?

The Environmental Protection Agency (EPA) proposed its new rule for regulating greenhouse gas (GHG) emissions for newly constructed power plants. Originally proposed in March 2012 with a standard threshold of 1,000 pounds of carbon dioxide (CO_2) equivalent per megawatt hour, the new source performance standards set a limit for new coal-fired power plants of 1,100 pounds of CO_2 equivalent per megawatt-hour (or 1,000–1,050 pounds over a seven-year period), 1,000 pounds of CO_2 per megawatt-hour for larger gas-fired plants, and 1,100 for smaller ones.

If Congress is serious about job creation and economic growth, it should drive back the regulation of GHGs. The massive regulatory costs will either be passed on to American families and businesses or offset by cuts in operations and investment—or both. Whatever the result, it will be economically injurious with futile results in impacting climate change. Congress can contain the damage by limiting either the EPA's authority or its budget to implement the regulations.

Climate Change Realities

The EPA has no explicit statutory authority to regulate CO_2 as a pollutant. But environmental activists, in conjunction with several states and cities, convinced the U.S. Supreme Court in *Massachusetts v. EPA* that CO_2 and five other GHGs may be regulated under the Clean Air Act. The majority made no recommendation as to whether the EPA *should* regulate CO_2; it simply ruled that it *could*.

The underpinning of the agency's GHG regulations is an "endangerment finding": the formal determination by the agency in 2009 that GHGs "cause or contribute to air pollution which may be reasonably anticipated to endanger public health or welfare." Of course, CO_2 emissions have no direct impact on human health. But the EPA concluded that man-made CO_2 emissions' warming effect would create more floods, hurricanes, droughts, and other natural disasters.

In preparing its finding, the EPA failed to follow federal data quality standards, and its conclusions about health effects are unsupported by clinical studies or toxicological data that regulators typically rely upon to discern risk. The agency's own inspector general concluded that "it is clear that EPA did not follow all required steps for a highly influential scientific assessment. We also noted that documentation of events and analyses could be improved."

Although there is a near unanimous consensus that the earth has warmed, no consensus exists regarding climate sensitivity, the role CO_2 plays with respect to climate change, whether global warming is a problem or a benefit, or how current temperatures fit into the broader climate context.

Climate models failed to predict the 16-year plateau in global temperatures, and droughts, floods, and hurricanes have not increased with increasing global CO_2 emissions. Understanding climate sensitivity and the immediate effects of how a doubling of CO_2 would affect world temperatures is far from complete, but new research indicates that the estimates were too high and need downward revision.

Higher Costs for Families

America has 497 billion tons of recoverable coal, which is enough to provide electricity for 500 years at current consumption rates. The EPA's new rule will effectively ban the construction of new coal-fired power plants, because the average coal-fired power plant emits nearly 1,800 pounds of carbon emissions per megawatt-hour. Even the newest, most efficient, super-critical power plant in West Virginia emits 1,700 pounds per megawatt-hour.

The only way for new coal-fired plants to meet the regulation is with carbon capture and sequestration (CCS) technology, which has challenges in terms of scalability, liquid CO_2 storage, and cost. The fact that the Clean Air Act stipulates that new source performance standards must reflect "the best system of emission reduction" as adequately demonstrated by the EPA administrator raises questions as to whether CCS meets this standard. Even if CCS were affordable, it does not justify the EPA's regulation, since regulation is intended to address a non-problem. CCS should be built only if companies believe it is in their economic interest to do so, such as for aid in oil extraction.

Taking away such a vital energy source will drive up energy prices for families and businesses. As energy prices increase, the cost of making products rises. Higher operating costs for businesses will be reflected in higher prices for consumers. The combination of higher prices and less disposable income for families will reduce employment and economic growth.

To make matters worse, the GHG regulations promulgated by the EPA will have no effect on climate change, a fact acknowledged by former EPA administrator Lisa Jackson and most recently by current administrator Gina McCarthy.

In a recent House Energy and Commerce Committee hearing, McCarthy said that EPA actions would not solve any climate problems but stressed that the U.S. needs to be a leader to attract international commitment. But if the U.S. leads on this issue, the countries that would make a difference in reducing global emissions are highly unlikely to follow. GHG emissions in China, India, and the rest of the developing world are rapidly increasing as economic growth expands, and those governments have no intention of curtailing that growth to mitigate a hypothetical risk. There are proposals for 1,200 coal-fired power plants worldwide, and China and India account for 818 of them.

Urging developing countries to curb their economic growth to reduce carbon emissions is immoral, as these countries are attempting to lift their citizens out of poverty and have more pressing environmental issues, such as obtaining breathable air and clean drinking water, neither of which CO_2 reduction will address.

Rein in the EPA

The most effective approach to such harmful, bureaucratic regulatory undertakings would be to permanently prohibit any federal regulators from using GHG emissions as a reason to regulate economic activity. Congress should reform federal policies and regulations to prevent unelected officials from implementing GHG regulations. Recommended actions include:

- Retracting the endangerment finding and establishing standards of scientific review for reconsideration by the agency,

- Prohibiting the EPA and other agencies from regulating GHG emissions unless expressly authorized to do so by Congress, and

- Prohibiting the EPA and other agencies from using any funds to promulgate or enforce any regulation intended to reduce GHGs.

Periodical and Internet Sources Bibliography

The following articles have been selected to supplement the diverse views presented in this chapter.

Jonathan Bernstein	"There Is No Republican Civil War," *Bloomberg View*, April 7, 2014.
Leigh Ann Caldwell	"In GOP Civil War, an Outsized Advantage," CNN, April 27, 2014.
Eleanor Clift	"How Tea Party Hero Jan Brewer Saved Obamacare in Arizona," *Newsweek*, June 19, 2013.
Linda Feldmann	"Campaign Kickoff: Can Republicans Win on Obamacare Alone?," *Christian Science Monitor*, March 6, 2014.
Ben Goad and Megan Wilson	"Republican Draws Line on Climate Regs," *The Hill*, February 6, 2013.
Elias Isquith	"Tea Party Secedes: The GOP Civil War Is Over, and So Is the GOP," *Salon*, October 11, 2013.
Abby D. Phillip	"Republicans and Tea Party Activists in 'Full Scale Civil War,'" ABC News, December 12, 2013.
Jason Sattler	"The Republican 'Civil War' Isn't About Policy: It's About Cash," *Huffington Post*, February 17, 2014.
Luiza Ch. Savage	"The Elephant in the Room: As Obama Falters, Republicans Are Too Busy Squabbling with One Other to Notice They're Missing Opportunities," *Maclean's*, March 16, 2014.
Javier H. Valdés	"House Republicans Would Be Foolish Not to Pass Comprehensive Immigration Reform," *Christian Science Monitor*, October 3, 2013.

OPPOSING
VIEWPOINTS®
SERIES

CHAPTER 4

What Issues Surround the Tea Party?

Chapter Preface

The right-wing Tea Party movement has been a major force in Republican politics since the congressional elections of 2010. Despite its importance, however, many commenters have argued that it is a myth—that there is not really a Tea Party at all. For example, Gary Younge in a November 7, 2010, article for the *Guardian* argues,

> The "Tea Party" does not exist. It has no members, leaders, office bearers, headquarters, policies, participatory structures, budget or representatives. The Tea Party is shorthand for a broad, shallow sentiment about low taxes and small government shared by loosely affiliated, somewhat like-minded people.

In other words, the Tea Party is just a rebranding of right-wing Republicans. To support his point, Younge points out that most Tea Party politicians, such as Christine O'Donnell of Delaware who won the 2010 Republican primary before losing in the general election, were around before the Tea Party label existed, and they merely attached themselves to it.

An October 2, 2013, editorial at the Truthout website makes a related point, arguing that the Tea Party is not a grassroots movement of citizens concerned about spending but is instead the creation of a small number of billionaires. Truthout says that one group, Americans for Prosperity, funded by wealthy brothers Charles and David Koch, "actually bussed Tea Party 'activists' around the country to protest President Obama's healthcare law."

Other writers, though, have insisted that the Tea Party is a real phenomenon that connects strongly to the lives of many people. Stanley Kurtz in an August 1, 2011, article at *National Review Online* says that the Tea Party's success shows that it is not, as many media outlets claim, simply the creation of a few wealthy donors. "Mainstream-media hatred for the Tea Party is still around, of course," he says. "But at least we now take it for granted that the Tea Party exists. In today's media culture, that's progress."

Lauren Fox in a February 27, 2014, article in *U.S. News & World Report* interviewed attendees at a rally for the Tea Party in Washington, DC, on the fifth anniversary of the movement. She notes that Tea Party events "still attract large and energetic crowds from all corners of the country," suggesting that there is ongoing support and a real constituency for Tea Party events.

In the end, it is likely true that the Tea Party is not an entirely new force in politics. It is a diffuse label that describes a rightward trend in the Republican Party rather than a sharply defined group. However, that is not the same as saying that it is a myth. Rather, as the label has become better known, people have begun to identify themselves with it. The Tea Party may not quite have existed before the term "Tea Party" became widely used, but the group surely does exist now.

The following chapter explores questions surrounding the Tea Party, such as whether the Tea Party hurts Republicans and whether it is based in religious beliefs or economic resentments.

> "The Tea Party, in other words, is that inner voice that speaks to us when things go wrong—the conscience of the nation at a crucial point in our history."

Tea Partiers Won't Go When Fun Ends

Ed Feulner and Sen. Jim DeMint

Ed Feulner is a former president of the Heritage Foundation; Jim DeMint is a former senator from South Carolina and the current president of the Heritage Foundation. In the following viewpoint, they argue that the Tea Party is in the best traditions of America and is fighting for the vision of the Founding Fathers. They argue that the Tea Party and its goals are broadly popular and that it will be a force for good in American politics for many years to come.

As you read, consider the following questions:

1. What sorts of concerns do the authors say Tea Partiers raise?

2. What previous examples of popular movements do the authors compare to the Tea Party?

3. Why do the authors say that Obamacare should be repealed but not immediately replaced?

In only 21 months the Tea Party has exploded from a handful of scattered, spontaneous rallies into a full-fledged national movement capable of throwing out incumbents. Challenging entrenched Washington habits, it is a force both parties must reckon with.

Skeptics and opponents, however, continue to ask two basic questions. First, does the Tea Party have any real philosophical depth, a historical pedigree? Second, will its force dissipate after the elections?

In short, critics accept that the Tea Party has a present—but they question whether it has a past and a future.

Yes and yes. Yes, the Tea Party has a pedigree as old as our nation, and yes, we think it is likely to continue to play a significant role in politics after Nov. 2. People in both parties who hope to wish it away and continue business as usual had better think twice.

Americans have been disappointed by leaders in both parties who campaigned to right past wrongs and then, after getting to Washington, cared more about power than promises. Tea Party supporters care more about principle than party labels or politics.

Tea Party members voice the kinds of concerns that even some of President Barack Obama's former supporters are beginning to raise. As one Obama voter asked the president at a recent town hall, "Is the American dream dead for me?"

These are the questions Americans are asking nationwide—in their kitchens, church halls and ballparks. These are the concerns expressed at Tea Party rallies everywhere.

The Tea Party seeks answers to such questions not in the dictates of Washington today but in our country's founding principles. There, it finds a prescription for constitutional, limited government based on God-given rights—not a Utopian blueprint for bureaucratic-managed change.

The Tea Party, in other words, is that inner voice that speaks to us when things go wrong—the conscience of the nation at a crucial point in our history.

What has gone wrong is clear. The "stimulus" package has failed to get this country back on its feet. The latest unemployment figures show that we still have anemic growth and nearly 10 percent unemployment. As Americans suffered, Washington wasted its time on a gargantuan, unmanageable and unaffordable health care package. No wonder many Americans feel frustrated.

But underneath the frustration, the Tea Party has roots that are deeper and aim higher. Deeper because it is within the best tradition of popular movements in our history—from the Great Awakening that gave rise to the American Revolution to the conservative revival that helped elect Ronald Reagan. Higher because it aims to recover our moral compass, bequeathed by our founders and preserved ever since.

The Tea Party also symbolizes Americans' indomitable desire for a better life. It reminds us that we're a country of free people who understand that liberty is fragile and must be vigilantly defended.

Some past grassroots movements have succeeded, and others have failed. Success comes because the energy of the moment is translated into a lasting, governing philosophy consistent with the settled opinions of the American people.

On this score, prospects look good. The Tea Party isn't about to go away after the November elections. Its powerful message of limited government is likely to remain a sharp thorn in the side of those in both parties who want to continue politics as usual.

Take Obama's health care package, which Tea Partiers have labeled "Obamacare." Obama and Democrats rammed this through Congress, against the wishes of a majority of the American people.

But the repealing legislation should not itself contain some new massive health care plan. Even if the legislation offers good policy, the Tea Party is here to remind Republicans that pushing large, unexamined bills through Congress is wrong. We need to repeal Obamacare immediately, then openly debate and pass conservative-drawn, sensible and broadly supported health care reform.

It's no surprise that pollsters Scott Rasmussen and Doug Schoen found that more than "half of the electorate now say they favor the Tea Party movement, around 35 percent say they support the movement, 20 [percent] to 25 percent self-identify as members of the movement and 2 [percent] to 7 percent say they are activists."

This means that all those protesters with their Constitutions at Tea Party rallies nationwide represent millions of fellow Americans. The answers they seek won't be found in the thousands of pages of new legislation coming out of Washington.

They are in those documents that first defined this nation and provide the most just framework for a free people to work hard, play by the rules and succeed.

> *"The Tea Party has extracted some very high costs from the party from which it will be difficult to recover."*

The Tea Party Hurts the Republican Party

Julian Zelizer

Julian Zelizer is a professor of history and public affairs at Princeton University and the author of Governing America: The Revival of Political History. *In the following viewpoint, he argues that Tea Party extremism has hurt the Republican Party. He says that Republican Tea Party candidates defeated more centrist opponents in primaries, allowing Democrats to win seats in the general election they otherwise would have lost. He also says Tea Party refusal to compromise has made it difficult for Republican leaders to legislate, which has further alienated moderates. He concludes that one of the biggest challenges facing the Republicans today is Tea Party extremism within the party.*

As you read, consider the following questions:

1. Which Tea Party candidates does Zelizer specifically say damaged Republican election chances?

2. According to Zelizer, why were Republicans unwilling to negotiate on a budget grand bargain in 2011?

3. What voting blocs does Zelizer say the Tea Party has alienated?

Back in 2010, the conservative columnist and CNN contributor David Frum was worried about what he saw in his own party. Frum, who had worked as a speechwriter for President George W. Bush, feared that Republicans would be tempted by Tea Party Republicans to shift far to the right to achieve short-term electoral gains that would cost the party in the long run.

"A party must champion the values of the voters it already has," Frum wrote, then warning, "But it must also speak to the votes it still needs to win."

High Costs

For several years, the Tea Party helped energize a moribund Republican Party. After the 2008 election, with conservatives reeling from the dismal approval ratings of Bush and the defeat of [2008 candidate] John McCain, Tea Party activists injected some life into the Republican grass roots, bringing out voters in the primaries who were frustrated with the political status quo.

They pushed the GOP [Grand Old Party, another name for the Republican Party] to focus more on the issue of deficit reduction and government spending, while creating immense pressure on the congressional leadership to avoid compromises. The midterm elections of 2010 put President Barack Obama on the defensive and constrained him for much of his first term.

But Frum was right about the long run. The Tea Party has extracted some very high costs from the party from which it will be difficult to recover. The most immediate cost was control of the Senate. In 2010 and 2012, Tea Party activists knocked out some powerful Republican candidates who probably would have been victorious and improved the chances for the party to win a majority in the Senate.

In 2010, the nation was riveted when Christine O'Donnell defeated U.S. Rep. Michael Castle in Delaware in the GOP primary. Most agree Castle would have won the Senate seat. O'Donnell could not. The seat went to a Democrat.

Nevada's Sharron Angle and Colorado's Ken Buck suffered similar fates. This year, powerhouse Sen. Richard Lugar of Indiana was defeated by Richard Mourdock, who uttered some explosive comments about abortion that fueled perceptions the GOP was far right. Democrats won the seat.

Besides the Senate, the electoral costs were also evident in the Republican presidential primaries, when Mitt Romney felt the need to make the kinds of "severely conservative" statements that cost him enormously in the election.

The Tea Party Republicans also made it difficult for Republicans to sign off on a $4 trillion "grand bargain" about taxes and spending when Obama's back was to the wall in 2011.

The most zealous Republicans were unwilling to capitulate to the president on the issue of tax increases in return for the spending cuts they sought. They gambled that Americans would elect a Republican in 2012, which would give them free rein on Capitol Hill.

But things turned out quite differently. Instead, Republicans don't have control of the White House and face the possibility of taxes going up for all taxpayers, as well as steep cuts in defense, if nothing is done.

They don't have the leverage that existed in the post-2010 election. By most indications, they will now have to settle for ending some of Bush's tax cuts and possibly domestic spending cuts that are not as deep as they could have gotten a few years ago.

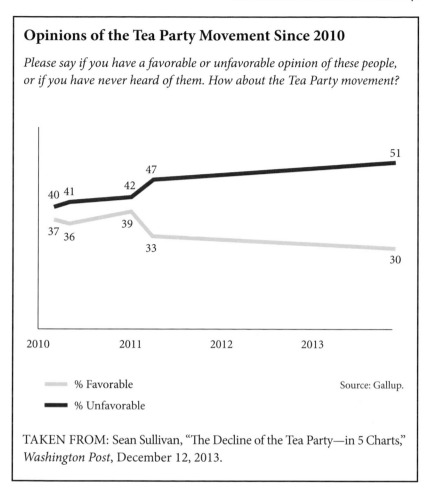

Opinions of the Tea Party Movement Since 2010

Please say if you have a favorable or unfavorable opinion of these people, or if you have never heard of them. How about the Tea Party movement?

40 41   42   47   51

37 36   39   33   30

2010   2011   2012   2013

    % Favorable   Source: Gallup.
    % Unfavorable

TAKEN FROM: Sean Sullivan, "The Decline of the Tea Party—in 5 Charts," *Washington Post*, December 12, 2013.

If the automatic cuts go through, a product of the failure to reach a deal when the wind was at their backs, conservatives will see heavy reductions on defense, something not likely to please the Republican base. Even if an acceptable deal goes through, after the 2012 election Americans will likely see Obama as the driving force and Republicans taking a deal because they didn't have any other choice.

Problems of Governance

The Tea Party has also undermined efforts by the GOP to position itself as the party of governance rather than the party of extremism.

The Tea Partiers are part of a dynamic in the party, that started with Barry Goldwater's run in 1964, which pushed out moderates and made it more difficult for the Republicans to build a long-term coalition, as Geoffrey Kabaservice documents in his book *Rule and Ruin.*

The demand to remain ideologically pure has consistently pushed Republican leaders to move to avoid saying yes to almost anything, preventing House Speaker John Boehner and Senate Minority Leader Mitch McConnell from cutting deals.

The inaction of the GOP and the ideologically charged rhetoric from its members have played directly into arguments by scholars such as Thomas Mann and Norman Ornstein that the GOP is moving far to the right and is responsible for the dysfunctional state of politics in Washington.

Finally, the Tea Party is making it increasingly difficult for Republicans to win over hugely important voting blocs that can play a major role in 2016 and 2020.

In 2012, the Republicans paid dearly among Latino voters for the rising power of hard-line anti-immigration advocates. The Tea Party helped to drown out voices such as those of Bush who believed the party needed to broaden its appeal and reach out to new constituencies, not shrink its electoral map. They have also turned off many younger millennial voters, another key constituency finding less to like about the Republican Party.

All of these point to the ways in which the embrace of the Tea Party has taken its toll on the Republicans. Recently, observing the losses that resulted from Tea Party candidates, Frum asked: "Have we learned our lesson yet?"

The answer is uncertain. At a moment when the party needs to avoid an electoral free fall with more red states turning blue, or at least becoming swing states, party leaders need to do some hard thinking about whether one of their greatest challenges does not come from Democrats, but from within.

> *"This 'end times' worldview is a foundational precept of the evangelical movement, from which many of the so-called Tea Party favorites spring. Scholars call it apocalypticism."*

The Tea Party Is Based in Apocalyptic Religious Beliefs

Joe McLean

Joe McLean is a political strategist who worked on the leadership team of Barack Obama's successful US Senate race. In the following viewpoint, he argues that Tea Party Republicans believe that the end of the world is coming and that they are in a struggle against the forces of evil led by Barack Obama and liberals. As such, they are unwilling to compromise and are more interested in purity than in policy goals or the health of the Republican Party. McLean says that Republicans who care about their party must confront Tea Party members. He believes the Tea Party will eventually be marginalized within the Republican Party or else the Republican Party will split into moderate and far-right wings.

As you read, consider the following questions:

1. Who does McLean name as the modern-day "apocalyptic prophets"?

2. What is Christian Dominionism, and what is Ted Cruz's connection to it, according to McLean?

3. Who does McLean believe might be receptive to the message of a modern "Whig Party"?

Want to know why the Tea Party [is] so eager to grievously wound the Republican Party? The answer is as simple as it is counterintuitive: Its leaders view themselves as modern prophets of the apocalypse.

Deliberate Destructiveness

In the aftermath of the great government shutdown of 2013, the Tea Party continues to cause heartburn for establishment Republicans. Consider the results of last week's elections [in November 2013], which offer clues to the internecine GOP [Grand Old Party, another name for the Republican Party] battles that lie ahead. Although it's much too early to draw hard conclusions, Chris Christie proved that a moderate, commonsense Republican could win in deep blue New Jersey, while in purple Virginia the wild-eyed social reactionary Ken Cuccinelli failed to gain traction outside his uber-conservative Christian-right base.

Yet the Tea Party is willing to defy overwhelming negative public opinion, wreck the government, risk plunging the world economy into chaos and invite political defeat. The driving force behind this destructive strategy is that Tea Party zealots answer to a "higher calling."

They believe America teeters on the brink of destruction, and hold as an article of faith that liberals, gays, Democrats, atheists and the United Nations are to blame. This "end times" worldview is a foundational precept of the evangelical movement, from which many of the so-called Tea Party favorites spring. Scholars call it apocalypticism.

Apocalyptic Prophets

Of course, the Tea Party is not just composed of members of the Christian right. Many are genuine libertarians. Some nurse an unreconstructed Confederate grudge, while others harbor a thinly disguised racism. However, the real energy, the animating force for the movement comes from evangelicals, of whom [Texas senator] Ted Cruz, [Minnesota congresswoman] Michele Bachmann and [former vice presidential candidate] Sarah Palin are the most strident. These are the modern-day "apocalyptic prophets."

Although the issues are secular, the prophets' anti-Obamacare [referring to the Patient Protection and Affordable Care Act] rhetoric rings with religious, end-times cadences. So to understand why they invoke chaos, we need to know where their ideas about an "apocalypse" came from.

Most theologians, including the revered Albert Schweitzer, believe John the Baptist and Jesus of Nazareth were Jewish apocalypticists. Simply put, these first-century prophets believed they were living in the "end times" before God would send his representative, the "Son of Man" (taken from a rather obscure passage in the Book of Daniel), to overthrow the forces of evil and establish God's justice on earth. Apocalypse literally translates as "the revealing" of God's will. For these early prophets the Kingdom of God was not to be a church, but a military and political kingdom on earth.

Lest this sound far-fetched to modern ears, listen to our modern Tea Party prophets in their own words:

> "You know we can't keep going down this road much longer. We're nearing the edge of the cliff. . . . We have only a couple of years to turn this country around or we go off the cliff to oblivion!"—Ted Cruz at the Values Voter Summit, Oct. 11

> "... I'm a believer in Jesus Christ, as I look at the End Times scripture, this says to me that the leaf is on the fig tree and we are to understand the signs of the times, which is your ministry, we are to understand where we are in God's End Times history. Rather than seeing this as a negative ... we need to rejoice, Maranatha Come Lord Jesus, His day is at hand. And so what we see up is down and right is called wrong, when this is happening, we were told this, that these days would be as the days of Noah. We are seeing that in our time."—Michele Bachmann, Oct. 5, 2013

> "And this administration will been [sic] complicit in helping people who wants [sic] to destroy our country."—Louie Gohmert on the floor of the U.S. House

> "The biggest war being waged right now is against our religious liberties and traditional values."—Rep. Tim Huelskamp, Values Voter Summit

> "The fight for religious freedom starts here at home because we are one nation under God."—House Majority Leader Eric Cantor, Values Voter Summit

For these apocalyptic prophets, the issues aren't even political anymore; they're existential, with Obamacare serving as the avatar for all evil. In this construct, any compromise whatsoever leads to damnation, and therefore the righteous ends justify any means.

Populism

Much of the prophets' message is couched in populist language. It sounds familiar to us because we've heard it all before. Historically, whenever our country has experienced economic stress an angry, reactionary vein of populism surfaces. Sometimes called "Jacksonian" [after President Andrew Jackson], this common thread actually reaches back to the American Revolution, then to Shays' Rebellion [an armed uprising in 1786–1787], through Jackson's [campaign slogan] "Augean Stables" to William Jennings Bryan's rants against science in the Scopes "Monkey Trial." It includes "Know-Nothings," Anti-Masons and [Louisiana governor and populist orator] Huey Long's "Every Man a King." George Wallace stood in the schoolhouse door [to prevent desegregation in Alabama in 1963] and [independent candidate] Ross Perot sabotaged George Bush the Elder's re-election [in 1992]. Except for Andrew Jackson, each burst of populist fervor ended badly.

Our modern prophets are fundamentally different. Their dogma springs from [evangelical leaders] Pat Robertson and Jerry Falwell, through James Dobson's Family Research Council, to the eerily omnipresent [Christian organization the] Fellowship and its C Street house.

Ted Cruz's father, Rafael, was seen in recently uncovered videos calling for America to be ruled by "kings" who will take money from anyone who is not an evangelical Christian and deliver it into the hands of fundamentalist preachers and their acolytes. This movement is called "Christian Dominionism," and it has many adherents in the evangelical right. It is also obviously and dangerously anti-democratic. These new apocalyptic prophets, and the demagogues who profit (pun intended) from them, see themselves locked in mortal combat against the Anti-Christ in a fight for America's soul—and wealth.

Now if you are battling the forces of evil for the very survival of the nation, there can be no retreat, no compromise, and no deals. Like the Jewish zealots at Masada, it's better to commit glorious suicide than make peace with the devil. There can be no truce with the Tea Party because its apocalyptic zealots can never take "yes" for an answer.

Since the apocalyptists cannot compromise, they must be beaten. President Obama and congressional Democrats seem to have finally grasped this fact, and are learning how to deal with them. By refusing to knuckle under to extortion in the government shutdown drama, Obama exposed their reckless radicalism and won resoundingly.

Republicans Must Confront the Tea Party

But Democrats can't solve this problem alone. To bring any semblance of order back to the American political system and restore a functioning two-party system, the GOP has to find its own equilibrium. Thankfully, this process has already begun.

Establishment Republicans, corporate CEOs [chief executive officers] and Wall Street moguls stand appalled at the Tea Party monster they helped to create. Formerly cowed into silence, they are beginning to see the handwriting on the wall and speak out against the self-destructive zealots.

In conservative Virginia, Ken Cuccinelli was largely abandoned by the GOP establishment. Many Republican leaders even went so far as to endorse the Democrat, Terry McAuliffe. Unable to raise significant money from the Republican establishment, Cuccinelli was outspent more than ten to one. While Virginians rejected a conservative who believes government's role is to regulate morality, New Jersey voters chose a conservative Republican [Chris Christie] who believes government has a constructive, practical role to play.

The contrast is striking—and instructive. Until Republicans slug it out among themselves and decide which kind of party they want to be, we will continue to lurch from crisis to crisis.

This family fight will not be easy or bloodless. The Tea Party represents roughly one-half of the Republican base. They love Cruz, Palin and the chorus of other voices crying in the wilderness. They are unified in their hatred of Obama, and they are organized down to the precinct level. More importantly, they despise the moderate voices in their own party.

Apocalyptic Counterculture

Invocations of the apocalyptic can be found within various religious traditions from the early days of European colonization of North America through the twentieth century and beyond. The great irony of American history is that the religious movement of Christian fundamentalism—relatively marginalized by the mainline denominations during the latter nineteenth century and the first half of the twentieth century—managed toward the end of the twentieth century to trump the death of God through a strange ideological admixture that juxtaposed millenarian anticipation of the end times and antipathy toward government, and nevertheless came to exercise an extraordinary influence in mainstream American cultural and political life. However, this surge did not occur in isolation from other apocalyptic developments.

Conservative American religion gained energy in the turbulent 1960s and '70s in part as a countermovement to the second broad channel of apocalypticism in the West—the counterculture and antiwar movements. Indeed, some within the conservative movement—radical elements of the antiabortion movement and Christian survivalists—eventually mimicked the bombings and assassinations initiated by some groups in the New Left, just as the conservative movement more generally adopted certain New Left social movement strategies and tactics.

John R. Hall, Apocalypse:
From Antiquity to the Empire of Modernity.
Malden, MA: Polity Press, 2004, p. 156.

Gerrymandered congressional districts guarantee many safe Tea Party seats. Powerful think tanks and advocacy groups like the Heritage Foundation, the Chamber of Commerce, American Enterprise Institute and others, which in years past underpinned the Republican establishment, are now heavily invested in the right-wing agenda and will not be easily co-opted. Deep-pocketed militants like the Koch brothers [David and Charles] will keep the cash flowing, and right-wing talk-radio heads will whip up the aggrieved faithful.

Two Outcomes

It's almost impossible to predict how this family fight will end, but there are at least two possible outcomes.

First, the pragmatists win. The Grand Old Party could be led out of the wilderness by a charismatic figure à la Chris Christie, who is viewed as a straight-talking, practical problem-solver. Any such leader will have to arise outside Washington. The pragmatists' backers would include big business, Wall Street, the military-industrial complex, GOP lobbyists and a plethora of wealthy patrons who can't afford any more Tea Party shenanigans.

They have a strong case. Moderates have won some dramatic conservative victories over the years, delivering massive tax cuts, reforming welfare, deregulating Wall Street, diluting *Roe v. Wade*, reviving federalism with block grants and reshaping today's conservative Supreme Court.

Second, the hard-liners revolt. The party splinters, and out of the wreckage a new center-right "Whig Party" emerges. This is not so far-fetched as it may seem. A recent bipartisan polling by NBC and *Esquire* magazine reveals a wide plurality: 51% of Americans view themselves as centrists, not deeply invested in either party.

Not surprisingly, these moderates have both liberal and conservative views. 64% support gay marriage, 63% support abortion in the first trimester, 52% support legalizing marijuana, and they support a strong social safety net by wide margins. But 81% support offshore drilling, 90% support the death penalty and 57% are against affirmative action. So a new moderate coalition might well attract significant support from the moderate middle, establishment Republicans, independents and centrist Democrats too.

Unfortunately for the apocalyptic prophets, only 29% of the moderate middle thinks churches or religious organizations should have any role at all in politics. So like the prophets of old, they seem fated to join that long sad procession of failed zealots and martyrs who were overwhelmed by hard reality and their own rigid dogma.

> "He was channeling the unfocused cul-
> tural rage of the principal body of his
> constituents: predominantly white,
> lower-middle-class Americans who feel
> 'disrespected' because the main currents
> of American life, economically, demo-
> graphically and culturally, are passing
> them by."

The Tea Party Is Based in Economic Class Resentments

Mike Lofgren

Mike Lofgren is a former Republican US congressional aide and the author of The Party Is Over: How Republicans Went Crazy, Democrats Became Useless, and the Middle Class Got Shafted. *In the following viewpoint, he argues that the Tea Party is fueled by middle-class economic and class resentments. He says that elites have bankrolled the Tea Party movement but that its strength resides in an alienated underclass that is angry at cul-tural shifts and its unstable economic standing. He says that the upper class has lost control of the movement, thus explaining the confusion and struggles for power within the Republican Party.*

As you read, consider the following questions:

1. Lofgren says that the Tea Party comports itself in ways inconsistent with the idea that it is composed of economic elites. What behavior in particular is Lofgren singling out?

2. What did Richard J. Evans write, and how does Lofgren link that book to the Tea Party?

3. What evidence does Lofgren provide that elite businesspeople sometimes make political miscalculations?

We read in the aftermath of the government shutdown and near default on the country's sovereign debt that the US Chamber of Commerce is clutching its pearls. "We are going to get engaged," said a mouthpiece for the chamber. "The need is now more than ever to elect people who understand the free market and not silliness." The chamber is the top lobbying organization in America, and it gave 93 percent of its political contributions to Republican candidates in the 2010 election that birthed the congressional Tea Party Caucus. Apparently it is now having buyer's remorse. *Politico*, the newsletter of the Beltway illuminati, reports similar tidings: Rich Republican mega-donors like hedge fund vulture Paul Singer are expressing frustration with Republican office holders, even though Singer has been a major financial backer of the Tea Party–oriented Club for Growth, which egged on the politicians who forced the shutdown. Even the Koch brothers [David and Charles] have been distancing themselves from the shutdown.

Roots of the Tea Party

Most Democrats, needless to say, are rubbing their hands with glee, and predictions of doom for the GOP [Grand Old Party, another name for the Republican Party] are too numerous to count. The Tea Party, according to this narrative, has taken over the Republican Party and will lead it to inevitable electoral oblivion: The sheer irrationality of their demands constitutes electoral suicide. Others are not so sure. Michael Lind has advanced the theory that the Tea Party is an aggregation of "local notables," i.e., "provincial elites [disproportionately Southern] whose power and privileges are threatened from above by a stronger central government they do not control and from below by the local poor and the local working class." He links it to a neo-Confederate ideology that is "perfectly rational" in terms of its economic objectives—a stark contrast to the prevailing description of the Tea Party as irrational. Lind further contends that progressives have misread the Tea Party, downplaying the element of elite control and obsessing over the anger and craziness of its followers.

There is some truth in this. The Tea Party definitely is disproportionately Southern, as Lind stipulates, and any movement that seeks to hobble the functioning of the federal government naturally will advance themes and tactics that sound a lot like the template of the Confederacy: states' rights, disenfranchisement of voters, use of the filibuster and so forth. Some Tea Party candidates look an awful lot like neo-Confederate sympathizers. But Lind misconstrues some of the data. If, as he says, 47 percent of white Southerners express support for the Tea Party, how does that square with his "local notables" theme: That the "backbone" of the movement is "millionaires [rather than] billionaires"? It is doubtful that 47 percent of the white population in the poorest region of the country consists even of local notables, much less millionaires.

That a fair number of local big shots is involved in the movement is unsurprising and natural, given their economic interests; what is more interesting from a sociological point of view, as well as more significant from a political perspective, is the millions of non-rich people, including those dependent on federal programs like Social Security and Medicare, who pull the lever for Tea Party candidates. The fact that 144 of 231 voting Republican House members opted for shutdown and default is not explained by the Svengali-like influence of a relatively small, regionally based group of Lind's "second-tier" affluent people, especially because the first tier, the people that the U.S. Chamber of Commerce represents, was opposed strongly to the shutdown and to allowing a default. The most plausible answer is that there is a mass popular movement (albeit working in carefully gerrymandered congressional districts) that would throw these members of Congress out of office if they had voted otherwise. If big-shot money were the sole criterion, the office holders would never have threatened default in the first place.

In advancing his thesis that Tea Party adherents are more affluent and more educated than average, Lind cites a *New York Times*/CBS News poll from early 2010 that claims those findings. This poll is frequently quoted in characterizations of the Tea Party, and there has been relatively little work done on the demographics of the movement since then. But one study found slightly lower levels of education in GOP congressional districts than in the country as a whole. Given the paucity of reliable data, it is not unreasonable to use GOP district demographics as a rough surrogate for Tea Party demographics if 62 percent of House Republicans are voting the Tea Party line on shutdown and default.

Not Elite

While it may be true that the Tea Party was originally about fiscal issues and initially attracted more affluent people, what appears to have happened is that the religious right, always on the lookout to infiltrate and take over organizations (see your local school board) gradually became the demographic center of gravity of the movement. That would explain why the Tea Party initially described itself as wholly concerned with debt, deficit and federal overreach but gradually became almost as theocratic as the activists from the religious right. If anything, they were even slightly more disposed than the rest of the Republican Party to inject religious issues into the political realm. According to an academic study of the Tea Party, "[T]hey seek 'deeply religious' elected officials, approve of religious leaders' engaging in politics and want religion brought into political debates." A glance at the bios of the steering committee for Tea Party Unity suggests a strong theocratic bias. That probably explains why Tea Party darling [Texas senator] Ted Cruz took time from obstructing Senate proceedings to be the marquee speaker at the Values Voter Summit, whose straw poll he won handily. There is plenty of anecdotal evidence of low-church zealotry, rather than typical plutocratic manners and mores, to be gained simply by watching Tea Party protests. Economic elites just might comport themselves like this, this, this, this or this when publicly expressing their political views, but—with the possible exception of [businessman] Donald Trump—I doubt it.

It is more likely that however the Tea Party initially presented itself, it is no longer a group of mainly affluent, well-educated people whose primary obsessions are the deficit, debt or health care policy. This became evident in the later stages of the shutdown, when it was obvious that Tea Party–influenced office holders had no coherent strategy for achieving concrete, tangible political goals. This confusion was memorably expressed by Rep. Marlin Stutzman, a Tea Party favorite: "We're not going to be disrespected. We have to get something out of this. And I don't know what that even is."

As Dr. [Sigmund] Freud knew, sometimes we say more than we intend. While the media collectively pounced on Stutzman's ignorance of his goal, they did not ask why he did not have a goal that he could express. And they let pass his comment about being "disrespected," an *idee fixe* of outsiders like teenage gang members who have self-esteem issues. Stutzman could not articulate a policy goal because he did not have one that he could utter. He was channeling the unfocused cultural rage of the principal body of his constituents: predominately white, lower-middle-class Americans who feel "disrespected" because the main currents of American life, economically, demographically and culturally, are passing them by. This accounts for the fevered, emotional, irrational tenor of their complaints, a hyperbolic resentment that cannot be explained by the fact that the federal budget is not in balance or that the [Patient Protection and] Affordable Care Act is costly and creates an unwieldy bureaucracy—features that did not seem to concern them when the Medicare prescription drug act passed in 2003 under a Republican administration. It also explains the weird preoccupations, such as denying contraception to women and rolling back legal protections for children, of North Carolina Republican Mark Meadows, a Tea Party caudillo who helped lead the charge to shut down the government. None of those preoccupations are on the agenda of the wealthy funders of the Tea Party; rich Republicans have a tendency to be socially somewhat liberal, or at least more socially liberal than the Republican voting base. For the wealthy, delving into private consensual matters is at best a distraction from their own preoccupation with maintaining their economic hegemony over society and, at worst, as in the case of the Tea Party voters' fixation with Obama's alleged foreign birth, it is a positive embarrassment.

Authoritarianism of the Lower Middle Class

In periods of political crisis or threatening social change, the lower middle class often has been the demographic segment most susceptible to militant authoritarian movements—such as the [Ku Klux] Klan or the Coughlinites [followers of Charles Coughlin] in earlier times in American history. In other countries as well, the lower middle class has been the basis of fascist movements. As Richard J. Evans documents in *The Coming of the Third Reich*, the original electoral backbone of the National Socialists [Nazis] was the lower middle class, exemplified by petty shopkeepers, the lower rungs of the white-collar professions and land-poor farmers. As the great economic calamity of 1929 intensified, these groups feared, above all, sinking into the despised proletariat. It was this emotion that caused them to identify the source of their problems less in the banks, corporations and cartels that were the proximate cause of the crash than in the contaminating presence of foreigners and the underclass. France has had periodic bouts of this phenomenon, with movements like Action Française, the post–World War II Poujadists (the definitive small shopkeepers movement) and, more recently, the anti-immigrant party of Jean-Marie Le Pen, whose psychologically penetrating political catchphrase was "I say what you are thinking." Capitalists are of course more than willing to fund such parties if they are on the brink of success and can be useful to capital, just as the German cartels began to fund the Nazis after their breakthrough election in September 1930. Nothing succeeds like success: University professors and intellectuals flocked to the Nazi Party once it gained power. But the motivating energy of the movement sprang, above all, from the fear and resentment of those tenuously situated a couple of rungs above the actual poor.

Lind will have none of this. In a follow-up piece further advocating his thesis, he takes swipes against those who see cultural deformations among ordinary people as a strong factor in the rise in authoritarian movements. Every critic of reactionary populism—Max Weber, H.L. Mencken, Richard Hofstadter, Theodor Adorno, C. Wright Mills—comes in for scorn as being a sniffish elitist. But Mencken's (and some of the others') disdain for the Southern Baptists and Methodists of the day certainly had a basis in fact, given that these organizations had plunged America into the long national nightmare of Prohibition, as well as having revived the Ku Klux Klan. And it is nothing other than Weber's "status politics" (meaning politics closely entwined with cultural issues) rather than purely elite economic concerns that explains the slogan "take back our country!" Populism certainly has had its progressive aspects. But in attempting to salvage a populism—particularly Southern populism—that does not have some seriously debilitating flaws, Lind overshoots the mark.

Lind provides data that do not really make his case. He cites a PRRI [Public Religion Research Institute] poll as follows: "White working-class voters in households that make less than $30,000 per year were nearly evenly divided in their voting preferences (39% favored Obama, 42% favored Romney). However, a majority (51%) of white working-class voters with annual incomes of $30,000 or more a year supported Romney, while 35% preferred Obama." He construes this as proof that the extreme rightward tilt of the GOP (of which the Tea Party is mostly the symptom, rather than the cause) is a result of the work of wealthy elites. Certainly the elites have bankrolled the Tea Party up to this point; only a fool would deny it. But that would not translate into more than a few percent of the vote if people in quite modest circumstances were not prepared to vote for Tea Party policies. If nearly 40 percent of white working-class voters making less than $30,000 a year (with many of them eligible for government income maintenance programs) were willing to vote for Romney, who famously expressed his disdain for "the 47 percent," that is significant. Regardless of the official poverty line, an annual income less than $30,000 represents straightened circumstances. By his own admission, Romney should not have carried anything more than a negligible percentage of these voters. And the fact that an actual majority of white working-class voters making more than $30,000 per year voted for Romney is the clincher. Had they represented all of America, Romney would have won comfortably. Unfortunately the PRRI poll does not indicate the upper bound of incomes for those persons, but people likely would not describe them-

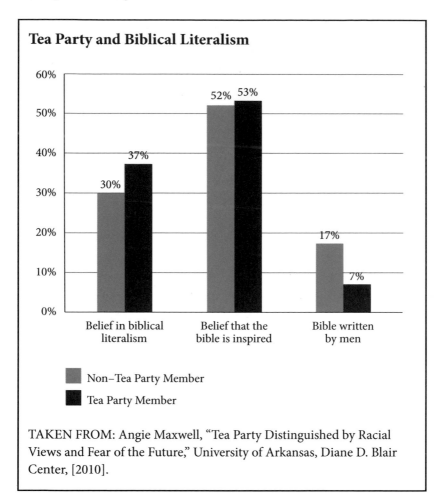

Tea Party and Biblical Literalism

TAKEN FROM: Angie Maxwell, "Tea Party Distinguished by Racial Views and Fear of the Future," University of Arkansas, Diane D. Blair Center, [2010].

selves as working class if they were making six-figure incomes. And we may assume anyone described as working class would not be one of Lind's "local notables."

The Mass Psychology of Fascism

Many observers have puzzled over the tendency of Tea Party adherents to favor policies that are often directly counter to their economic interests: Why would a disproportionately older group that is accordingly more dependent of Social Security and Medicare opt for candidates who want to "reform entitlements" (i.e., privatize Social Security and voucherize

Medicare)? This line of analysis dates in its contemporary American form to Thomas Frank's *What's the Matter with Kansas?*, in which he marveled at this self-defeating syndrome. He located the source of the problem in the cultural anxieties that have driven the culture wars of the past 40 years and how cleverly the right wing and its business allies have exploited that anxiety. Frank identified the culture wars as trumping economics, but the fascinating question he never sufficiently answered is how this mechanism works at the granular level.

In 1933, psychologist Wilhelm Reich attempted to answer that question in *The Mass Psychology of Fascism*. His answer: The virus is all around us, because it is latent within ourselves. But it flourishes in rigid, punitive and authoritarian upbringings, whereby a person's early domestic circumstances foreshadow his future relationship with state and society. In a home life filled with punishments, taboos and guilt, Reich saw the kernel of the future fascist: repressed, conformist and outwardly submitting but filled with a rage over his humiliation whose source could never be admitted. This dilemma accounts for the curiously contradictory psychology of the adherents of authoritarian movements. They are highly suggestible followers of some strong leader whom they can masochistically adore, yet at intervals they become anarchic and rebellious. And as they cannot admit the roots of their rage, they displace it onto others: Hence the xenophobia, the militancy, the endless search for scapegoats. It is no coincidence that this kind of personality finds an outlet on the Tea Party—which overlaps so heavily with followers of the religious right, whose lives are often a catalogue of commandments, taboos and shibboleths.

All this unhealthy energy usually does not find a unified political objective unless coaxed along by money and organizational skill from outside. Frank's identification of business interests as the nurturers of cultural resentment for their own political and financial gain is of course correct, and we have seen this pattern more and more vividly illustrated since the 2004 publication of his book. But that thesis, which is now common knowledge, seems to implicitly assume that the business interests know what they are doing, and that the dupes are under the firm control of the plutocrats. As we have seen with the US Chamber of Commerce, the plutocracy has gotten more than it bargained for. Local business interests are beginning to be appalled by the berserker antics of Tea Party stalwarts like [Michigan representative] Justin Amash and [Utah senator] Mike Lee.

It was ever thus; there are always not a few businessmen willing to finance an ostensibly populist movement so as better to manipulate it, and who then get an unpleasant surprise. In the most infamous example, the German industrialists convinced themselves that it was so important to crack down on the left that it was worth holding their noses and bankrolling a déclassé Austrian corporal [that is, Adolf Hitler]. They could even tolerate him as chancellor; after all, he would be easily controllable because his cabinet had "sensible, pro-business conservatives" such as [Alfred] Hugenberg and [Franz] von Papen who would shape the new chancellor's intended policies in the preferred direction. But sometimes Frankenstein's monster does not respond to the commands of its master, and money does not invariably dictate the wayward course of ideas and emotions. In short, our elites, for all their Machiavellian wire-pulling, can be stupid and shortsighted.

> *"The battle over civil rights produced a rigidly homogenous and disproportionately Southern Republican Party, fertile grounds for the sort of purity contest you see consuming the South today."*

How Racism Caused the Shutdown

Zack Beauchamp

Zack Beauchamp is editor of TP Ideas and a reporter for the ThinkProgress blog. In the following viewpoint, he argues that the racial divisions of the slavery and civil rights eras created the conditions for the present-day Tea Party movement. The movement of conservative whites into the Republican Party was driven by Democrats' embrace of civil rights. This same division, he says, has been responsible for moving the South further and further toward the Republican Party. Thus, Beauchamp concludes, while the Tea Party is not opposed to health care reform because it was proposed by a black president, the increasing conservatism and unwillingness to compromise of the Republican Party has been fueled by ongoing racial divisions from the era of segregation.

As you read, consider the following questions:

1. According to Beauchamp, why was Franklin Roosevelt forced to stay out of the anti-lynching fight?

2. How did conservative ideology provide a rationale for resisting integration after 1964, according to Beauchamp?

3. How did Southern elites contribute to a national conservative move in the Republican Party?

This isn't an article about how Republicans shut down the government because they hate that the president is black. This is an article about how racism caused the government to shut down and the U.S. to teeter on the brink of an unprecedented and catastrophic default.

I understand if you're confused. A lot of people think the only way that racism "causes" anything is when one person intentionally discriminates against another because of the color of their skin. But that's wrong. And understanding the history of the forces that produced the current crisis will lay plain the more subtle, but fundamental, ways in which race and racism formed the scaffolding that structures American politics—even as explicit battles over race receded from our daily politics.

The roots of the current crisis began with the New Deal—but not in the way you might think. They grew gradually, with two big bursts in the 1960s and the 1980s reflecting decades of more graduated change. And the tree that grew out of them, the Tea Party and a radically polarized Republican Party, bore the shutdown as its fruits.

How the New Deal Drove the Racists Out

In 1938, Sen. Josiah W. Bailey (D-NC) filibustered his own party's bill. Well, part of his party—Northern Democrats, together with Northern Republicans, were pushing a federal anti-lynching bill. Bailey promised that Southern Democrats would teach "a lesson which no political party will ever again forget" to their Northern co-partisans if they "come down to North Carolina and try to impose your will upon us about the Negro:"

> Just as when the Republicans in the [1860s] under-took to impose the national will upon us with re-spect to the Negro, we resented it and hated that party with a hatred that has outlasted generations; we hated it beyond measure; we hated it more than was right for us and more than was just; we hated it because of what it had done to us, because of the wrong it undertook to put upon us; and just as that same policy destroyed the hope of the Republican Party in the South, that same policy adopted by the Democratic Party will destroy the Democratic Party in the South.

Bailey's rage at the affront to white supremacy was born of surprise. Until 1932, the South had dominated the Democratic Party, which had consistently stood for the South's key regional interest—keeping blacks in literal or figurative fetters—since before the Civil War.

But the Depression-caused backlash against Republican incumbents that swept New Yorker Franklin Roosevelt into the White House and a vast Democratic majority into Congress also made Southerners a minority in the party for the first time in its history. The South still controlled the most influential committee leadership votes in Congress, exercising a "Southern Veto" on race policy. The veto forced FDR to stay out of the anti-lynching fight ("If I come out for the anti-lynching bill, [the Southerners] will block every bill I ask Congress to pass to keep America from collapsing," he lamented).

The veto also injected racism into the New Deal. Social Security was "established on a racially invidious, albeit officially race-neutral, basis by excluding from coverage agricultural and domestic workers, the categories that included nearly 90 percent of black workers at the time," University of Pennsylvania political scientist Adolph Reed Jr. wrote in the *Nation*. "Others, like the [Civilian Conservation Corps], operated on Jim Crow principles. Roosevelt's housing policy put the weight of federal support behind creating and reproducing an overtly racially exclusive residential housing industry."

Yet, Reed notes, the New Deal not only benefited blacks, but brought them to a position of power in the Democratic Party. "The Social Security exclusions were overturned, and black people did participate in the WPA, Federal Writers' Project, CCC and other classic New Deal initiatives, as well as federal income relief," he reminds us. "Black Americans' emergence as a significant constituency in the Democratic electoral coalition helped to alter the party's center of gravity and was one of the factors—as was black presence in the union movement—contributing to the success of the postwar civil rights insurgency."

Hard evidence of the Northern Democrats' radicalization on civil rights, outflanking the GOP, can be found by the early 1940s. UC-Berkeley's Eric Schickler and coauthor Brian Feinstein built a database of state party platforms from 1920–1968 and examined their positions on African-American rights. They found that "the vast majority of non-southern state Democratic parties were clearly to the left of their GOP counterparts on civil rights policy by the mid-1940s to early 1950s." African-Americans and other sympathetic New Deal coalition constituencies, like Jews and union leaders, deserve the bulk of the credit—these new Northern Democrats made supporting civil rights a litmus test for elected Democratic officials. That explains why, from the early New Deal forward, congressional Northern Democrats voted more like Northern Republicans than their Southern brethren on civil rights.

Schickler and Feinstein pair the shift on civil rights to the parties' broader post–New Deal ideological shifts. New Deal liberalism's vehement support for government intervention in the economy made Democrats more open to the sorts of intrusive economic regulations, like desegregating private businesses, that civil rights campaigners demanded. Meanwhile, "the GOP's ties with chambers of commerce, manufacturers' associations, real estate groups, farm lobbies, and other organizations opposed to the increased government oversight of private enterprise that would come with fair employment and other civil rights legislation encouraged the GOP's drift toward racial conservatism." As Speaker of the House Joe Martin (R-MA) told an assembly of black Republicans in 1947:

> I'll be frank with you: we are not going to pass a [non-discrimination in private business bill], but it has nothing to do with the Negro vote. We are supported by New England and Middle Western industrialists who would stop their contributions if we passed a law that would compel them to stop religious as well as racial discrimination in employment.

Republican economic libertarianism, together with its gradual embrace of traditionally Southern "states rights" arguments as weapons in the war on the New Deal, set the stage for the eventual white flight from the Democratic Party.

And Southern Democrats, without whose votes the New Deal never could have happened, were willing to sacrifice their commitment to economic liberalism on the altar of white supremacy. Historian Ira Katznelson, whose 2013 work *Fear Itself* focuses on the role of Southern Democrats in the New Deal, analyzed congressional votes from 1933 to 1950 to better understand the political alliances of the time. Katznelson and his coauthors focus on the votes of Southern Democrats on six issues: "planning, regulation, expansive fiscal policies, welfare state programs, a national labor market and union prerogatives, and civil rights."

The Southerners, as Democrats, strongly supported the first four, but bucked the Northern wing of the party on the last two. But why labor in addition to civil rights? Katznelson et al. find a precipitous drop-off in Southern support for pro-labor laws during World War II, one of the two key reasons being that "wartime labor shortages and military conscription facilitated labor organizing and civil rights activism." "Labor market and race relations trends and issues," they found, had become "conjoined." For Southern Democrats, racism trumped liberalism.

Hence the famous Dixiecrat revolt of 1948, when Strom Thurmond and like-minded Southerners temporarily seceded from the Democratic Party over Harry Truman and the Democratic platform's support for civil rights. The tacit bargain that Katznelson documents during the Roosevelt administration, in which the Northern Democrats would get their New Deal if the Southern Democrats got their white supremacy, became untenable.

But the Dixiecrats weren't ready to migrate en masse to [the] Party of Lincoln just yet. Something needed to happen to make the Republican Party shed its commitment to leading on civil rights wholesale. That "something" was the rise of the modern conservative movement.

'The Great White Switch'

Earl Black and Merle Black are twin brothers. Both are political scientists at (respectively) Rice and Emory University. The twins, frequent coauthors, are widely considered to be the deans of the study of Southern politics.

In their book *The Rise of Southern Republicans*, the Blacks pinpoint two key transition points for Southern whites when the trends we've already seen produced truly marked change.

By the 1950s, the splits between Northern and Southern Democrats in Congress had become irreconcilable. The party's leadership was "refusing to call party meetings" for fear of catastrophe.

The Southern Democrats had to form alliances with the more conservative wing of the Republican Party. In a reverse replay of the South's deal with Roosevelt and Northern Democrats, the Blacks found, Southern Democrats helped Republicans fight Truman's economic policy while Republicans protected the Southern right to filibuster, allowing them to retard progress on civil rights without alienating black voters by voting against any particular piece of civil rights legislation. This "Inner Club" of Southern Democrats and conservative Republicans "informally set the limits on passable legislation."

But it wasn't until Barry Goldwater and the rise of the modern conservative movement that this marriage was formally consummated. Goldwater lost all but six states—Arizona, his home, and five Deep South states. It was the first time the GOP had prevailed at the presidential level in the South in the party's history. Republicans have held the South since.

Goldwater, a Sun Belt senator who believed in integration, seemed like an odd choice to inspire Southerners to leave LBJ [President Lyndon B. Johnson], a Texan with a storied racist past. But that surface level analysis entirely misses the role of the Goldwater-led conservative movement in the Southern imagination.

By the Johnson-Goldwater election, it had become clear that overt racism and segregationism was politically doomed. *Brown v. Board of Education* and LBJ's support for the 1964 Civil Rights Act saw to that. As this scary recognition dawned on Southern whites, they began searching for a new vehicle through which to shield themselves and their communities from the consequences of integration. The young conservative movement's ringing endorsement of a minimalist federal government did the trick—it provided an on-face racially neutral language by which Southerners could argue against federal action aimed at integrating lily-white schools and neighborhoods.

Kevin Kruse, a Princeton historian whose work focuses on the South and the conservative movement, finds deep roots in segregationist thought for this turn. "In their own minds, segregationists were instead fighting *for* rights of their own," Kruse suggests. These "rights" included "the 'right' to select their neighbors, their employees, and their children's classmates, the 'right' to do as they pleased with their private property and personal businesses, and, perhaps, most important, the 'right' to remain free from what they saw as dangerous encroachments by the federal government."

Kruse traces this language through white resistance to desegregation from the 40s through the 60s, using a detailed examination of "white flight" in Atlanta as a synecdoche. In the end, he finds, "the struggle over segregation thoroughly reshaped Southern conservatism . . . segregationist resistance inspired the creation of new conservative causes, such as tuition vouchers, the tax revolt, and the privatization of public services." The concomitant rise of the modern conservative movement and the civil rights movements' victories conspired to make Southern whites into economic, and not just racial, conservatives.

Kruse's theory isn't based on mere anecdote. M.V. Hood, III, Quentin Kidd, and Irwin L. Morris' book *The Rational Southerner* arrays a battery of statistical evidence correlating Southern whites' Republican turn with black voter mobilization. The more politically active blacks became, their data suggest, the more whites flocked to conservative Republicans as a counter.

So from 1964 on, conservative white Southerners voted against Democrats at the presidential level. But the *en masse* formal switch in party identification didn't happen until Reagan. "Reagan's presidency," Merle and Earl Black write, "was the turning point in the evolution of a competitive, two-party electorate in the South. The Reagan realignment of the 1980s dramatically expanded the number of Republicans and conservative independents in the region's electorate." The Blacks attribute this to a combination of Reagan's winning political personality and (more persuasively) the relative prosperity of the 1980s. Not only were white conservatives ideologically inclined to support Reagan's Republican Party, but they became wealthier on his watch.

Reagan-era conservatism also left behind the naked racism that had driven Southern Democrats out of the party, which the civil rights movement had rendered unacceptable. By 1983, even Strom Thurmond, the former Dixiecrat candidate for president, voted to make Martin Luther King, Jr.'s birthday a national holiday. Reagan-era conservatism, while hardly above race-baiting, became far more about foreign policy hawkishness, Christian-right style social conservatism, and—most importantly for present purposes—free market economics.

The South's conversion to movement conservatism led to local and congressional Republican victories throughout Dixie. These culminated in the Gingrich Revolution [after House Speaker Newt Gingrich] in 1994, when hard-line Southern conservatives took charge of the Republican congressional delegation, seemingly for good.

Sen. Bailey's prediction had finally come true. The Democrats' about-face on race cost them the South.

The Legacy of the Democratic South's Rebellion: The Tea Party

We all know what happens next. The Southern conservative takeover of the Republican Party pushes out moderates, cementing the party's conservative spiral. This trend produces

The Tea Party and Racism

At least one scholarly study suggests that problematic racial assumptions are widely held by Tea Party supporters. In a survey conducted in seven states by scholars at the University of Washington, Tea Party supporters tended to rate blacks and Latinos as less hardworking, less intelligent, and less trustworthy than did other respondents. Tea Partiers' views of minorities were even more extreme than other avowed conservatives and Republicans. Statistically, conservative Republicans tend to agree more than do non-conservatives with statements such as "if blacks would only try harder they could be just as well off as whites," but Tea Party supporters are even more likely than other conservatives to believe that racial minorities are held back by their own personal failings. It is important to note that, compared to other Americans, Tea Partiers rate *whites* relatively poorly on these characteristics, too. Tea Partiers have negative views about all of their fellow citizens; it is just that they make extra-jaundiced assessments of the work ethic of racial and ethnic minorities.

Theda Skocpol and Vanessa Williamson,
The Tea Party and the Remaking of Republican Conservatism.
New York, Oxford University Press, 2012, p. 69.

the Tea Party, whose leading contemporary avatar—Ted Cruz—engineers the 2013 shutdown and risk of catastrophic default.

So we can draw a tentatively straight line between the last 80 years of racial politics and this week's political crisis. Aside from being an interesting point of history, what does that tell us?

First, that the shutdown crisis isn't the product of passing Republican insanity or, as President Obama put it, a "fever" that needs to be broken. Rather, the sharp conservative turn of the Republican Party is the product of deep, long-running structural forces in American history. The Republican Party is the way that it is because of the base that it has evolved, and it would take a tectonic political shift—on the level of the Democrats becoming the party of civil rights—to change the party's internal coalition. Radicalized conservatism will outlive the shutdown/debt ceiling fight.

Second, and more importantly, the battle over civil rights produced a rigidly homogenous and disproportionately Southern Republican Party, fertile grounds for the sort of purity contest you see consuming the South today. There's no zealot like a new convert, the saying goes, and the South's new faith in across-the-board conservatism—kicked off by the alignment of economic libertarianism with segregationism—is one of the most significant causes of the ideological inflexibility that's caused the shutdown.

That's not to dismiss the continued relevance of race in the Southern psyche. There's no chance that, when 52 percent of voting Americans are over 45, the country has just gotten over its deep racial hang-ups. Read Ta-Nehisi Coates' masterful "Fear of a Black President" if you don't believe me.

Naturally, the South remains Ground Zero. One 2005 study that measured racial animus found that Southern whites were "more racially conservative than whites elsewhere on every measure of racial attitudes ordinarily used in national surveys." And Obamacare is a racially polarized issue. Brown University's Michael Tesler found, in 2010, that there was an astonishing 20 point higher racial gap on health policy in 2009 than there was in the early 90s. In Tesler's experiments, subjects' responses to statements about health policy were "significantly more racialized" when the statement was attributed to President Obama than President Clinton.

So it'd be implausible, to put it mildly, to say that modern racism has nothing to do with the shutdown fight. That being said, it's hard to pinpoint exactly what its role is, and it'd be overly simplistic to reduce the whole shebang to racial animus. One of historical racism's many political children—our right-polarized South—has to play an important role, one that's independent of ongoing racial prejudice.

The basic idea goes something like this. Southern white flight from the Democratic Party, motivated as it was by the compatibility of purist economic libertarianism with de facto segregation, produced *especially conservative Republicans*. This hard-line opposition to intervention in the marketplace survived the death of open segregationism, and as Southerners became more and more critical to the party's national fortunes, their brand of libertarianism gradually began to dictate the party's ideological agenda. Primaries enforced the party line nationally, driving out moderate non-Southern Republicans and making the party's representatives nationally fit the Southern-cast mold.

There's certainly suggestive evidence to this point. Take a look at this chart of trends in House DW-NOMINATE scores [not included]—a measure of a legislator's distance from the ideological mean of the time.

Notice how that sharp tick toward conservatism among Republicans starts around 1976, just when Southern whites were abandoning the Democratic Party in droves. At the same time, Southern Democrats start looking more and more like Northern Democrats (the story is basically the same in the Senate). It seems like Republicans became more conservative just as they were starting to become more Southern.

There's more. "After the 1994 elections, white Southern Republicans accounted for sixty-two members of the 230-member House GOP majority," Ari Berman writes in the most recent edition of the *Nation*. "Today, white Southern Republicans account for ninety-seven members out of the 233-

member House GOP majority." The percentage of Southerners in the GOP House caucus, Berman reports, has gone up in every election but one since 1976.

These Southerners also make up large percentages of the House's most conservative blocs. Though Southerners make up a little over 30 percent of the U.S. population and 42 percent of House Republicans, a full 60 percent of the House Tea Party Caucus is Southern. Southerners comprise 50 percent of the Republican Study Committee, the House "cabal" so powerful in the past three years that, according to *National Journal*, "the RSC's embrace or rejection of any legislative effort has become the surest indicator of whether it will pass the chamber." 19 of the 32 House Republicans the *Atlantic* deemed "most responsible" for the shutdown hail from the South.

Southern congresspeople voted consistently more conservatively than their Northern colleagues on the "fiscal cliff" deal that resolved the last debt ceiling standoff. Southern Republicans in more competitive districts, according to the *New Republic*'s Nate Cohn, voted more ideologically than Northern Republicans in *safe GOP districts.*

This shouldn't surprise anyone: The South has been setting the Republican agenda since the 1994 Gingrich Revolution, both at the congressional and the base level. Political scientist Nicol Rae conducted a series of interviews with House members in power from 1994–1998, finding that the "Southern members of the Republican class of 1994 have acted as the 'conscience' or 'keepers of the flame' of this Republican revolution." The enduring consequence, according to Rae, was finalizing the long-term demographic trends that were making the Southern bloc into "the dominant element, regionally, ideologically, and culturally in the congressional GOP."

As the Southern faction became the face of the GOP in the mid-90s, the GOP's electorate became a lot more conservative nationally. Panel data reviewed by Alan Abramowitz and Kyle Saunders found that, from 1992–1996, ideological conservatives joined the Republican Party in droves. That's because Southern elites played a key "signalling" role; their prominent national conservatism signaled to conservatives around the country that the Republican Party was theirs.

Penn's Matthew Levendusky, who literally wrote the book on conservatives "sorting" themselves into the Republican Party, says that "even when the data are consistent with a nationalization hypothesis, the South still played a crucial role in the sorting process because of the key role of Southern elites." As conservative Southern elites took over the Republican Party, hyper-conservative Americans followed, becoming the GOP primary voters we know and love today.

So, to sum up: The South's race-inspired conversion to radical conservatism made the GOP pure enough to threaten default over Obamacare in two distinct ways. First, Southern elected leaders are simply more conservative than other Republicans, and are making up a larger and larger percentage of total Republican seats in the House. Second, Southern elites send out signals that drive out moderate primary voters throughout the country, making even non-Southern Republicans more conservative.

In *Dinotopia*, a famous children's book, the residents of a fictional dinosaur-human city use a water clock shaped like a helix. It's a reflection of their novel concept of time. Instead of thinking of the passage of time as either linear or cyclical, they see it as a spiral: History forever repeats itself, but with new, unpredictable twists tossed in.

It's a neat metaphor for the role of North-South conflict in the United States. The basic cleavage between North and South, began by slavery, has set the fault lines of American politics again and again. This time, the crisis isn't as severe as the civil war, nor as divisive as the battle over civil rights. But make no mistake: Today's Republican radicalism, with all of its attendant terrifying brinksmanship, is the grandchild of the white South's devastating defeats in the struggle over racial exclusion.

| "Black Tea Party members dispute racist claims, and being on the inside, they'd know better than some pundits brainwashed in the echo chamber of liberal elitism."

The Tea Party Is Not Racist

Noel S. Williams

Noel S. Williams is a writer for the American Thinker. *In the following viewpoint, he argues that mainstream media falsely accuse the Tea Party of racism. He says that black Tea Party members attest to the fact that the movement is not racist and that demographically the makeup of the movement is similar to the makeup of America. He argues that the Tea Party supports hard work and universal values and that it promotes the kind of liberty Martin Luther King Jr. advocated. Williams concludes that it is Democrats and liberals who focus on race and are therefore the real racists.*

As you read, consider the following questions:

1. How does Obama encourage racial division, according to Williams?

2. According to Williams, how does Marco Rubio's personal story undermine charges that the Tea Party is racist?

3. What African American advances does Williams list?

Despite repeated attempts in the media to portray the Tea Party as racist, their recruitment and polices actually benefit minorities.

Liberal Elitist Bigotry

Ironically, the MSM [mainstream media] turns a color-blind eye toward President Obama, who may be the most racially divisive president in history.

Some Tea Party anger is racist—that was the moronic accusation from jaded political analyst Cokie Roberts on MSNBC the other day. Of course, most large organizations will have some unsavory elements, including the Democrat Party, but the Tea Party really is color-blind.

Cokie's mind-set is endemic in the MSM and propagated by a narcissistic president whose temperament is tainted by racial hubris. President [Barack] Obama tacitly encourages his media minions to accuse political dissenters of racism. So let's refute these diabolical claims because the Divider-in-Chief, who promised he'd be "post-racial" and transcend race, actually descends into sordid racial politics for political expediency.

Charges of racism are the last refuge of liberal elitist bigotry. But black Tea Party members dispute racist claims, and being on the inside, they'd know better than some pundits brainwashed in the echo chamber of liberal elitism. Actually, Tea Party demographics are rather mainstream, and more accurately reflect our societal makeup than the failing [liberal] Occupy Wall Street movement [protesting economic inequality]. Surprisingly, more blacks support the Tea Party than Occupy Wall Street.

Two prominent Tea Partiers are Texas GOP [Grand Old Party, another name for the Republican Party] senator Ted Cruz and Florida's Marco Rubio—hardly part of the "White Establishment" [since both are Latino]. I'd bet my car they're more inclusive than many limousine liberals; I'd bet my house they're less racist than many of the Congressional Black Caucus.

During his Cruz-athon to delay Obamacare [referring to the Patient Protection and Affordable Care Act], Cruz passionately reminded us that you don't see people boarding boats in the Florida Keys heading to Cuba. No, the traffic is all the other way—from Cuba to America.

Rubio then took to the Senate floor to provide his compatriot some support under the guise of lengthy, convoluted questions. He described how his family, who also fled from Cuba, drove around nice neighborhoods in the U.S. admiring the opulence. Instead of wallowing in envy, his parents encouraged Marco to work hard and take personal responsibility so he could participate in the American dream.

Hard Work and Initiative

That's the simple key—hard work and personal initiative. In such a vast and diverse nation, we might all encounter injustice at some time—discrimination or pernicious reverse discrimination. But racism is not so systematic anymore that hard work and initiative can't overcome the remnants of prejudice.

Most of us have profound policy disagreements with President Obama. That doesn't make us racist any more than when we disparage Senator Harry Reid's tactics in the continuing resolution debacle.

There're a priori reasons to believe that Tea Partiers have, and would, overwhelmingly support black luminaries like Alan Keyes, Herman Cain, or Dr. Ben Carson for political office. Indeed, favored Tea Party presidential contenders for

2016 include the following "minorities": Cruz, Rubio, [Louisiana] Gov. [Bobby] Jindal, and Dr. Ben Carson. Now tell me earnestly that the Tea Party is not color-blind!

The Tea Party and Progress

Beyond their makeup, Tea Party policies are actually more beneficial to minorities than President Obama's government-centric morass.

Consider the progress African-Americans have made over recent decades, and realize that Tea Party–type principles underpinned these developments. For example, protecting the voting rights of citizens; holding teachers accountable; sponsoring school choice; promoting regulatory and tax reform; disciplining the EPA [Environmental Protection Agency]; and encouraging innovation and free enterprise. All these Tea Party–endorsed positions will further these advances:

- In 1970, 1469 elected officials were black; that's now about 10,500.

- In 1964, 26% of blacks aged 25+ completed 4 years of high school; now much more.

- In the 2012 election, African Americans voted at a higher rate than whites.

- With buying power over $1 trillion annually, if African Americans were a country, they'd rank 16th.

- African Americans are by far the richest and freest blacks in the world. In fact, calculations of the GNP [gross national product] of black America would make it one of the richest "nations" in the world.

Ironically, Obama's big government approach and burdensome regulations have actually created wider racial disparities, particularly in unemployment. He's imprisoned by the notion that equality is a higher value than freedom. To invoke the spirit of [12th-century French political commenter] Alexis de

Tocqueville: Tea Party principles espouse equality in liberty; Obama would rather the socialist model of equality in servitude.

Former deputy assistant secretary of the interior David Cohen (of Samoan descent) highlights the irony that Obama's compulsion to forcibly "spread the wealth around," and to create government dependency in exchange for votes is actually harming minorities.

In his epochal "I Have a Dream" speech, [civil rights leader] Martin Luther King Jr. [MLK] refused to believe the bank of American justice was bankrupt; indeed, he demanded payment of the promissory note from America's vaults of opportunity. Clearly, the vaults of opportunity in our nation are now more easily opened, with Tea Party activists passing out the combination so all, regardless of race, can share MLK's dream. There's no promise of equality of outcomes, but plenty of collateral backing equality of opportunity.

That opportunity is leveraged by those who get off the dole and take personal responsibility for their future; in short, by those who espouse Tea Party programs. For while government assistance can temporarily help us overcome negative cash flow, prolonged dependence on welfare retards skill development, dulls the mind and stymies motivation to meet the terms of America's promissory notes of opportunity.

Tea Party antipathy is directed towards Obama's socialist policies, not the person. Their predilection is for freedom, applied equally, rather than languishing in mediocre equality. His dereliction in fostering success, in celebrating the American dream, will ensure mediocrity for all. Now who's racist, in practice if not in theory?

Periodical and Internet Sources Bibliography

The following articles have been selected to supplement the diverse views presented in this chapter.

Gail Russell Chaddock	"Why Did Tea Partyers Surrender? Because January Will Be Different, They Say," *Christian Science Monitor*, October 17, 2013.
Thomas R. Eddlem	"The War on the Tea Party," *New American*, February 17, 2014.
Linda Feldmann	"Is the Tea Party Running Out of Steam?," *Christian Science Monitor*, April 12, 2014.
Sandy Fitzgerald	"GOP Establishment: How Do We Blunt Tea Party Effect?," Newsmax, November 7, 2013.
Lauren Fox	"Tea Party Grows Up, but Remains Grass Roots at Its Core," *U.S. News & World Report*, February 27, 2014.
William A. Galston	"Profiling the Tea Party and Its Impact on the GOP," Brookings Institution, October 18, 2013.
John Halpin	"The Tea Party Is Killing the Republican Party," *ThinkProgress*, April 30, 2013.
Jeff Horseman	"Tea Party Hurts GOP, Poll Finds," *Press-Enterprise* (Southern California), December 4, 2013.
Josh Kraushaar	"The Tea Party's Over," *National Journal*, March 18, 2014.
Greg Sargent	"Tea Party Economics: A Long Term Loser," *The Plum Line—Washington Post* (blog), April 23, 2014.
Paul Waldman	"The Future of Tea Party-GOP Infighting," *Plum Line—Washington Post* (blog), April 23, 2014.

For Further Discussion

Chapter 1

1. Jonathan Chait argues that the Republican Party has not tried hard enough to reach out to minorities and that this will hurt the party in the long run. Harry J. Enten maintains that the Republican Party is gaining support among more and more white voters and that the party does not need to change demographics to win future elections. After reading both viewpoints, with which author do you agree, and why?

2. Jeremiah Goulka argues that voter ID laws disproportionately affect poor, minority voters who have trouble obtaining forms of identification and that Republicans push for these laws because they know it will hurt Democrats who are largely supported by minority constituents. Do you agree with Goulka's argument? Why, or why not?

Chapter 2

1. Sean Trende argues that Republicans do not need to appeal more to Hispanic voters to win in future presidential elections. He says that for Republicans to win the White House in 2016 they need to appeal to working-class white voters by nominating a candidate who has a populist stance on economics. Do you think this strategy can work for Republicans in the 2016 election? Why, or why not?

2. Fred Schwarz argues that Republicans do not need to tailor their message to appeal to women. He says that women are intelligent and should be presented with the same policy arguments as men. Mary Kate Cary, however, posits that Republicans need to improve their outreach to women. Which author do you think presents the stronger argument, and why?

3. Neil King Jr. introduces Russell Moore, a key member of the Southern Baptist Convention, the county's largest group of evangelicals, who historically vote Republican. Moore advises evangelicals to back off hot-button cultural issues such as abortion and same-sex marriage and to focus on job creation and education. Do you think evangelicals, and by extension Republicans, becoming more tolerant and inclusive in their message will help win over voters, particularly young voters? Explain.

Chapter 3

1. Tamar Jacoby argues that Republican support for immigration reform can help the party in the long run and will gain favor of the party with voters. Arnold Ahlert, however, argues that even if Republicans pass immigration reform, Hispanics will still distrust them and will not vote for them. With which author do you agree, and why?

2. Lanhee Chen argues that Republicans should stop fighting President Barack Obama's health care reform law and allow it to be implemented so voters can see for themselves the ill effects of the law. In your opinion, if Obamacare fails, will Republicans gain an electoral advantage from this? Explain your reasoning.

Chapter 4

1. Julian Zelizer argues that Tea Party extremism has hurt the Republican Party. Do you think he presents a strong argument to support this claim? If so, give examples from the viewpoint. If you do not think he presents a strong argument, explain how he could make a more convincing case.

2. Mike Lofgren argues that Tea Party constituents are mainly white, lower middle-class Americans who resent the wealthy, but it is the wealthy who financially support the Tea Party movement. He says that the upper class has

lost control of the movement, causing the Tea Party to struggle for power within its own party. Do you agree with Lofgren's take that the Tea Party is based in economic class resentment? Explain your reasoning.

3. Noel S. Williams argues that the Tea Party is not racist but rather supports hard work and promotes liberty for all people. How does Williams say the Barack Obama administration hurts minorities while the Tea Party promotes opportunity for all? Do you agree with the author? Why, or why not?

Organizations to Contact

The editors have compiled the following list of organizations concerned with the issues debated in this book. The descriptions are derived from materials provided by the organizations. All have publications or information available for interested readers. The list was compiled on the date of publication of the present volume; the information provided here may change. Be aware that many organizations take several weeks or longer to respond to inquiries, so allow as much time as possible.

American Enterprise Institute (AEI)
1150 Seventeenth Street NW, Washington, DC   20036
(202) 862-5800 • fax: (202) 862-7177
website: www.aei.org

The American Enterprise Institute (AEI) is a research organization dedicated to preserving limited government, private enterprise, and a strong foreign policy and national defense. The institute publishes the magazine the *American*, the current issue of which is available on its website. Also on its website, AEI publishes testimony, commentary, speeches, and articles, including "Rand Paul Won't Save the Republican Party," "George Bush's True Legacy?: A Republican Party in Denial," and "The Evolution of the Republican Party Voter."

Brookings Institution
1775 Massachusetts Avenue NW, Washington, DC   20036
(202) 797-6000 • fax: (202) 797-6004
website: www.brookings.edu

Founded in 1927, the Brookings Institution is a think tank that conducts research and education in foreign policy, economics, government, and the social sciences. The institution analyzes current and emerging issues and produces new ideas that matter for Americans and people worldwide. Its publications include the quarterly *Brookings Review* and periodic policy briefs, while its website offers links to articles such as "Did the Tea Party Help or Hurt the Republicans?" and blog posts such as "Libertarian Values & a Divide in the Republican Party."

Cato Institute

1000 Massachusetts Avenue NW
Washington, DC   20001-5403
(202) 842-0200 • fax: (202) 842-3490
website: www.cato.org

The Cato Institute is a nonprofit research center that approaches policy issues from a libertarian perspective with an emphasis on limited government and individual responsibility. While it analyzes a wide range of issues, the institute has produced several studies and research projects on government and politics in the United States. It has a large number of articles available on its website, including "Republicans Go from Daddy Party to Baby Party" and "A Republican Party for the Future."

Center for American Progress (CAP)

1333 H Street NW, 10th Floor, Washington, DC   20005
(202) 682-1611 • fax: (202) 682-1867
website: www.americanprogress.org

The Center for American Progress (CAP) is an independent think tank that works on twenty-first-century challenges such as energy, national security, economic growth and opportunity, immigration, education, and health care. CAP develops new policy ideas, critiques the policies that stem from conservative values, and challenges the media to cover the issues that truly matter. The group also produces numerous articles and policy papers and sponsors *ThinkProgress*, a blog that advances progressive ideas and policies. Blog posts on the Republican Party include "Where Have All the Moderate Republicans Gone?" and "Blow by Blow: A Comprehensive Timeline of the GOP's 4-Year Battle to Kill Obamacare."

Center for Responsive Politics

1101 Fourteenth Street NW, Suite 1030
Washington, DC 20005-5635
(202) 857-0044 • fax: (202) 857-7809
website: www.opensecrets.org

The Center for Responsive Politics is a nonpartisan, nonprofit research group that tracks money in politics and its effect on elections and public policy. The center conducts computer-based research on campaign finance issues for the news media, academics, activists, and the public at large. Its website contains up-to-date information, charts, and other data on federal elections in the United States. Its Politicians & Elections section contains information on the fund-raising and campaign financing activities for the Republican Party for congressional, senatorial, and presidential elections from 2000 to the present.

ConservAmerica

971 South Centerville Road, PMB 139, Sturgis, MI 49091
(269) 651-1808
website: conservamerica.org

ConservAmerica was founded in 1995 as Republicans for Environmental Protection. The organization aims to strengthen the Republican Party's platform on environmental issues and works to strengthen the party's efforts to conserve natural resources and protect the environment. ConservAmerica endorses Republican candidates who focus on natural resource conservation and environmental health and who seek bipartisan legislation to protect the earth. Its website features an In the News section as well as a blog that features posts such as "Why Wouldn't GOPers Like Renewable Energy" and "2014: The Year of the Republican Conservation Revival."

Heritage Foundation

214 Massachusetts Avenue NE, Washington, DC 20002-4999
(202) 546-4400

e-mail: info@heritage.org
website: www.heritage.org

The Heritage Foundation is a conservative public policy research institute that supports the principles of free enterprise and limited government. Its many publications include the monthly *Policy Review*, position papers, fact sheets, and reports. The foundation's website also features *The Foundry* blog, which includes entries such as "Does Obama Secretly Want Republicans Debating Immigration? This Conservative Thinks So," "In the Twitter Wars, Republicans Win," and "Conservatives to House Republicans: Do Nothing on Immigration Reform."

Hoover Institution
434 Galvez Mall, Stanford University
Stanford, CA   94305-6010
(650) 723-1754
website: www.hoover.org

The Hoover Institution at Stanford University is a public policy research organization that focuses on politics, the economy, and foreign affairs. Through publications such as the *Hoover Digest, Defining Ideas,* and *Policy Review,* as well as through research compiled by its task forces and working groups, the Hoover Institution provides information on a broad range of topics and works to influence American public policy. Its website offers position papers, op-eds, videos, blog posts, and articles such as "Demographics and the Future of the GOP," "The Future of the Tea Party," and "Rebuilding the Republican Brand."

National Federation of Republican Women (NFRW)
124 N. Alfred Street, Alexandria, VA   22314
(703) 548-9688 • fax: (703) 548-9836
e-mail: mail@nfrw.org
website: www.nfrw.org

The National Federation of Republican Women (NFRW) is a grassroots political organization with thousands of active members across the nation. The organization works to promote the policies of the Republican Party; elect Republican candidates; inform the public through political education and activity; and advance the effectiveness of Republican women in government. NFRW publishes the *Republican Woman* magazine and offers the *Capital Connection*, a weekly e-newsletter. Its website features a Women and the GOP section that provides a detailed history of women's role in the Republican Party and lists Republican women in leadership positions at the state and national level.

National Republican Congressional Committee (NRCC)
320 First Street SE, Washington, DC   20003
(202) 479-7000
website: www.nrcc.org

Founded in 1866, the National Republican Congressional Committee (NRCC) is dedicated to increasing the number of Republicans serving in the US House of Representatives. To this end, the NRCC provides financial contributions to Republican candidates and organizations; offers technical and research assistance; organizes voter registration and voter turnout initiatives; and participates in Republican Party–building activities. Its website features press releases, videos, and a blog with posts that include "New Poll: Obama, Dems and Obamacare Growing More and More Unpopular."

Pew Research Center
1615 L Street NW, Suite 700, Washington, DC   20036
(202) 419-4300 • fax: (202) 419-4349
website: www.pewresearch.org

The Pew Research Center is a nonpartisan "fact tank" that provides information on the issues, attitudes, and trends shaping America and the world. It conducts public opinion polls and social science research, reports and analyzes news, and holds forums and briefings, but it does not take positions on policy issues. The US Politics section on its website provides information, reports, and articles on a wide range of topics, including gun control, health care, immigration reform, the national economy, and voter demographics. Its articles on US political parties include "GOP Deeply Divided over Climate Change," "Tea Party's Image Turns More Negative," and "Whither the GOP? Republicans Want Change, but Split over Party's Direction."

Republican National Committee (RNC)

310 First Street SE, Washington, DC   20003
(202) 863-8500
website: www.gop.com

The Republican National Committee (RNC) formulates and promotes policies and positions of the Republican Party. It is responsible for organizing the Republican National Convention, the first of which was held in Philadelphia in 1856. The RNC's website includes information on party activities and campaigns and offers a detailed account of the Republican Party that includes a time line of noteworthy moments throughout party history. The RNC website also includes the *Chairman's Blog*, which offers posts such as "Why Democrats Are Worried, and What the RNC Is Doing," and the *GOP Blog*, featuring posts such as "RNC Launches '14 in 14' Women's Initiative" and "RNC Challenges White House to Answer Enrollment Questions."

Bibliography of Books

Joel D. Aberbach and Gillian Peele, eds.

Crisis of Conservatism?: The Republican Party, the Conservative Movement, and American Politics After Bush. New York: Oxford University Press, 2011.

Max Blumenthal

Republican Gomorrah: Inside the Movement That Shattered the Party. New York: Nation Books, 2009.

Charlie Crist and Ellis Henican

The Party's Over: How the Extreme Right Hijacked the GOP and I Became a Democrat. New York: Penguin, 2014.

Ross Douthat and Reihan Salam

Grand New Party: How Republicans Can Win the Working Class and Save the American Dream. New York: Anchor Books, 2009.

Mickey Edwards

The Parties Versus the People: How to Turn Republicans and Democrats into Americans. New Haven, CT: Yale University Press, 2012.

Robert Eugene Emanuel

G.O.P Black & Strong: African Americans and the Republican Party. Seattle, WA: CreateSpace, 2014.

Jonah Goldberg

Liberal Fascism: The Secret History of the American Left, from Mussolini to the Politics of Change. New York: Broadway Books, 2009.

Lewis L. Gould   *Grand Old Party: A History of the Republicans.* New York: Oxford University Press, 2012.

Howard Green   *Fools and Knaves: A Pragmatist's View of the Economic Warfare Being Waged by the Republican Party Against the Great American Middle Class.* Bloomington, IN: iUniverse, 2014.

Margaret Hoover   *American Individualism: How a New Generation of Conservatives Can Save the Republican Party.* New York: Random House, 2013.

Edward Hudgins, ed.   *The Republican Party's Civil War: Will Freedom Win?* Poughkeepsie, NY: Atlas Society, 2014.

Matthew W. Hughey and Gregory S. Parks   *The Wrongs of the Right: Language, Race, and the Republican Party in the Age of Obama.* New York: New York University Press, 2014.

Geoffrey Kabaservice   *Rule and Ruin: The Downfall of Moderation and the Destruction of the Republican Party, from Eisenhower to the Tea Party.* New York: Oxford University Press, 2013.

Ronald T. Libby   *Purging the Republican Party: Tea Party Campaigns and Elections.* Lanham, MD: Lexington Books, 2013.

Mike Lofgren — *The Party Is Over: How Republicans Went Crazy, Democrats Became Useless, and the Middle Class Got Shafted*. New York: Penguin, 2013.

Robert Mason — *The Republican Party and American Politics from Hoover to Reagan*. New York: Cambridge University Press, 2012.

Steven P. Miller — *Billy Graham and the Rise of the Republican South*. Philadelphia: University of Pennsylvania Press, 2009.

William J. Miller, ed. — *The 2012 Nomination and the Future of the Republican Party: The Internal Battle*. Lanham, MD: Rowman & Littlefield, 2013.

Chris Mooney — *The Republican Brain: The Science of Why They Deny Science—and Reality*. Hoboken, NJ: John Wiley & Sons, 2012.

Raulston B. Nembhard — *Beyond Petulance: Republican Politics and the Future of America*. Orlando, FL: Olde Wharf Publishers, 2014.

Barbara F. Olschner — *The Reluctant Republican: My Fight for the Moderate Majority*. Gainesville: University Press of Florida, 2013.

Rand Paul — *The Tea Party Goes to Washington*. New York: Center Street, 2011.

Scott Rasmussen and Doug Schoen — *Mad as Hell: How the Tea Party Movement Is Fundamentally Remaking Our Two-Party System.* New York: HarperCollins, 2010.

Heather Cox Richardson — *To Make Men Free: A History of the Republican Party.* New York: Basic Books, 2014.

Elliot A. Rosen — *The Republican Party in the Age of Roosevelt: Sources of Anti-Government Conservatism in the United States.* Charlottesville: University of Virginia Press, 2014.

Theda Skocpol and Vanessa Williamson — *The Tea Party and the Remaking of Republican Conservatism.* New York: Oxford University Press, 2013.

Bryan Hardin Thrift — *Conservative Bias: How Jesse Helms Pioneered the Rise of Right-Wing Media and Realigned the Republican Party.* Gainesville: University Press of Florida, 2014.

Timothy N. Thurber — *Republicans and Race: The GOP's Frayed Relationship with African Americans, 1945–1974.* Lawrence: University Press of Kansas, 2013.

Richard A. Viguerie — *Takeover: The 100-Year War for the Soul of the GOP and How Conservatives Can Finally Win It.* Washington, DC: WND Books, 2014.

Michael Wolraich   *Unreasonable Men: Theodore Roosevelt and the Republican Rebels Who Created Progressive Politics.* New York: Palgrave Macmillan, 2014.

Index

A

Abortion issue
  Conservative statements, 20
  Evangelical opposition, 85–86, 97
  gender belief differences, 79
  Mourdock, Richard, comments, 150
  Protestant opposition, 93
  Roe v. Wade decision, 79, 85, 160
  Southern Baptist opposition, 96
  support by moderates, 160
Abramowitz, Alan, 37, 185–186
Adams, Gordon, 14, 15
Adorno, Theodor, 168
Advancement Project (Ad.P), 51
African Americans
  2008–2012 voter turnout, 69 (table), 71
  Florida voters, 59, 62 (table), 63–64
  Tea Party candidates, 190–191
  views on immigration, 114 (table)
  voter identification laws, 45
  votes for Republicans, 40
The Age of Austerity (Edsall), 30
Ahlert, Arnold, 110–116
Akin, Todd, 19
Amash, Justin, 172
American Action Forum, 129
American Civil Liberties Union (ACLU), 53

American Enterprise Institute
  Brooks, Arthur C., leadership, 27
  right-wing agenda support, 160
  Ryan, Paul, tipping point speech, 28
  unmarried voter data, 76
Americans for Tax Reform, 132
Anderson, Jeffrey H., 122–126
Angle, Sharron, 19, 20
Asian Americans
  2008–2012 voter turnout, *69*
  Republican leanings, 56
Ayotte, Kelly, 16

B

Babington, Charles, 112–113
Bachmann, Michele, 155, 156
Bailey, Josiah W., 174–175, 181
Balanced Budget Amendment, 98
The Battle (Brooks), 27
Beauchamp, Zack, 173–187
Beck, Glenn, 99
Berman, Ari, 184–185
Bernstein, Jonathan, 16, 104
Black, Earle, 181
Black, Merle, 181
Boehner, John
  disinterest in immigration bill, 111
  frustration with Tea Party, 103, 152
  government shutdown comment, 118
  waiving of Hastert Rule, 107, 109

I

J

K

L

M